Learning to Sing in a Strange Land

Learning to Sing in a Strange Land

When a Loved One Goes to Prison

WESLEY F. STEVENS

WIPF & STOCK · Eugene, Oregon

LEARNING TO SING IN A STRANGE LAND
When a Loved One Goes to Prison

Wipf & Stock
A Division of Wipf and Stock Publishers
199 W. 8th Ave., Suite 3
Eugene, OR 97401
www.wipfandstock.com

ISBN 13: 978-1-59752-535-0

Manufactured in the U.S.A.

The inmates in the accounts of jail and prison written by Carolyn Stevens are not
identified by their real names.

To
GARY WHITBECK

Contents

Foreword

PRISONS ARE ALIEN PLACES of despair and destructiveness. Prisons are measures of fear and anxiety where we make invisible those who frighten us the most. On a closer look, of course, the ones in prison are real people, so like us with names and mothers and fathers and possibilities. We are invited by our faith to look closely beyond fear to notice names and persons with histories and hopes. It is because prisons hold persons loved by God that faith sends us always back to prison yet again:

1. It is reported that some were "prisoners in misery and in irons," but He shatters the doors of bronze, And cut in two the bars of iron (Ps 107:16).

2. It is anticipated by God's spirit that liberty is proclaimed to the captives and release to the prisoners (Isa 61:1).

3. It is commended that, "I was in prison and you visited me" (Matt 25:36).

4. It is remembered that in the vexed life of Paul and Silas, The jailer woke up and saw that the prison doors were wide open (Acts 16:27).

There is something about a prison in all its fearfulness that draws the attentiveness of the God of the gospel and that compels God's people.

The large narrative of the god of emancipation is the backdrop for the story that brought forth this book, a story of hurting and healing, of being away from home and coming home. It allows us to look inside the prison and to understand what it takes to live through a loved one's prison time in pain and grief, but not without hope.

I am fortunate to have been a bystander while this family hoped in active ways for their loved one's release. It was by happenstance—or by God's providential goodness—that through my work Wesley got in touch with the lament tradition of the book of Psalms. These ancient prayers of anguish and hope are characteristic of the faith of ancient Israel, even if they have been largely purged from contemporary Christian usage. These prayers are voiced by people who have no resource and who can see no way "out," but who pray tenaciously, demandingly, and hopefully. People who pray in this way find that candor before God's holy throne becomes a door to buoyancy and possibility. Wesley and his wife prayed that way and their daughter, Carolyn, for whom they prayed, now at last is free. It is "as though" their prayer has been answered; God has heard and acted, albeit through the slow, formal processes of review and parole. The outcome for all such agents of prayer is newness and beginning again. This story invites us into the particularity of a profound painfulness, through that particularity, moreover, we are invited into the company of God who dwells among prisoners and outside of prisons, both venues making all things new. This is the God:

> *who executes justice for the oppressed;*
> *who gives food to the hungry;*
> *the Lord sets the prisoners free.*
> *The Lord opens the eyes of the blind;*
> *the Lord lifts up those who are bowed down;*
> *the Lord watches over the strangers;*
> *he upholds the orphan and the widow.*
> —Ps 146:7–9b)

Walter Brueggemann
Columbia Theological Seminary
October 1, 2007

Introduction

By the rivers of Babylon, there we sat down, yea,
we wept when we remembered Zion.
We hanged our harps upon the willows in the midst thereof.
For there they that carried us away captive
required of us a song; and they that wasted us required of
us mirth, saying, Sing us one of the songs of Zion.
How shall we sing the Lord songs in a strange land?

—Psalm 137:1–4 (KJV)

PRISON IS A STRANGE land, a land of deep heartache and sadness. Over two million people are serving prison time in America. Millions more are carrying the mark of prison as those who were formerly incarcerated, including large numbers of men and women who have been released on parole. The negative influences of prison reach beyond the razor wire fences; they upset and sadden loved ones and friends who, in different ways, are also "doing time." The question of how to sing in the midst of such widespread captivity of body, mind, and spirit is one that finds answers in the testimonies of those who have wept in remembrance of "Zion."

This book was written as a consequence of my daughter, Carolyn, going to prison. She offers the most direct contribution to it through sharing her recorded observations and experiences of what it was like living in jails and prisons. Her life after prison, featuring the joys of home and her employment with a service-oriented organization, is a story of love and acceptance as remarkable in itself as how she was able to manage her time served in prison.

I have made extensive use of the Psalms because of my love of poetry and, more importantly, because of my timely discovery of Walter Brueggemann's thoughtful assessment of psalmic spirituality. Brueggemann's work afforded me a pastoral accompaniment through the places and perceptions of a loved one's imprisonment. I have concluded that without the poetry that "destabilizes all our settled 'facts' and opens the way for transformation and the gift of newness,"[1] the story of a loved one who was lost and then was found could not have been told with as much confidence in God's movement of love and power.

My wife, Marilyn, and I, along with our two children, six-year-old Carolyn and three-year-old Van, moved to the location of my new appointment as the Administrator of Holly Hall in January of 1971. This special Christian Retirement Community in Houston, Texas, provided us with a house on spacious grounds across Fannin Street from Houston's world famous Astrodome. The residents claimed Carolyn and Van as part of the Holly Hall family and lavished upon them an abundance of love and affection.

Many years later, we entered a time of disorienting sadness when Carolyn was placed in the Harris County Jail on criminal charges. Through the kind of trouble previously unknown to us in our relatively safe corner of the world, faithful friends became special agents of God's love whereby we were strengthened for the journey ahead. Then, as we moved into a wilderness of deep shadows, familiar songs of faith became, in the context of continuing sadness and uncertainty, spiritually substantive gifts.

Men and women with whom Marilyn and I shared the experience of having a loved one in prison touched our lives in ways that have influenced much of what I have written. We met them in the lines that formed outside the prison as well as in the prison visitation rooms. When we joined the Texas Inmate Families Association (TIFA), an organization devoted to helping family members who have loved ones in prison, the caring spirit of that company helped to make our journey through a strange land not quite so lonely. Words from the hymn, "Blest Be the Tie That Binds," describe how we felt about being with them through a common experience.

> We share our mutual woes, our mutual burdens bear;
> and often for each other flows the sympathizing tear.
>
> —John Fawcett

What we learned in helping Carolyn resulted, at length, in our acceptance of opportunities to help other families with loved ones in prison.

---

1. Brueggemann, *Finally Comes the Poet*, 5.

Then, in visiting with other prison inmates and taking advantage of opportunities to talk with prison officials, we were able to become more knowledgeable about prison life and what keeps prisons operating with high occupancy counts. Occasionally the signs of goodness and mercy found inside of prisons surprised us.

I am grateful to the special people who carry out the work of various ministries to prisoners for teaching me what the church is called to do on behalf of those whose lives have taken a wrong turn. Through all of the experiences we have had in this broad area of Christian discipleship, the two people who stand out most are Murray Batt who, through our own United Methodist denomination, introduced us to Emmett Solomon, Executive Director of the Restorative Justice Ministry Network.

Gary Whitbeck, an ordained minister who served as a pastor in the Central Texas Conference of the United Methodist Church until his official retirement in late December 2007, is a servant leader of understanding and compassion. As he visited Carolyn in prison during the entire length of her sentence, driving long distances each month from where his church was located, he ministered to all of us. In dedicating this book to Gary, I think of others like him who visit prisoners with whom they share, in special ways, the love of Jesus.

I cannot conclude this introduction without mentioning the residents of Holly Hall who inspired us with their love and care through all the years of Carolyn's incarceration. They were regularly informed about what was happening in our lives and their prayers revealed to God how much they cared for us. I am grateful, during these latter days, to be their minister and friend even as new faces in their number remind me of how quickly our time on earth passes.

Frederick Buechner offers this special insight concerning the value of remembering things that have brought sorrow into our lives.

> The sad things that happened long ago will always remain part of who we are just as the glad and gracious things will too, but instead of being a burden of guilt, recrimination and regret that make us stumble as we go, even the saddest things can become, once we have made peace with them, a source of wisdom and strength for the journey that still lies ahead.[2]

---

2. Buechner, *Telling Secrets*, 33. Copyright © 1991 Frederick Buechner. Reprinted by permission of HarperCollins Publishers.

I offer this writing as a sign of the peace I have made with the past and as a pledge to share such peace with those I meet who endure the heartache of having a loved one in prison.

1

In the Day of Trouble

The Lord answer you in the day of trouble!
The name of the God of Jacob protect you!

—Psalm 20:1

I WAS AWAKENED EARLY in the morning by the telephone ringing. I
picked it up and heard a recorded message telling me, "If you will accept a collect call from the Harris County Jail, don't hang up." I held for
a moment and then heard our daughter, Carolyn, say, "I'm in jail." After
a few seconds of complete silence, she said, "Please don't give up on me."
She was evasive when I asked, "Why?" She said something like, "It's a long
story" and "There are extenuating circumstances." After telling me not to
do anything until she could call again, I asked if we could get her out on
bail. She replied, "No, not now." Then she repeated the words, "Please don't
give up on me." In a state of painful disbelief, I replied, "We will do what
we can to help you."

Marilyn was at her mother's home not far away, assisting her mother
with a worsening illness related to congestive heart failure. When I called
her, I began by saying, "Carolyn is in trouble." Before she could reply, I said,
"She is in jail." A moment of silence was followed by questions that I could
answer only by repeating what Carolyn had just told me. We decided not
to call Van, Carolyn's brother, since he planned to be home in a few days
on spring break from his studies at Kansas University.

I went through the routine responsibilities of my work at Holly Hall
in a worried state of mind, keeping the news about Carolyn to myself and
trying not to appear anxious or distracted to the residents. After returning
to our house shortly after five p.m., I talked to Marilyn again. Expressions

of hope were exchanged between us that our daughter's trouble could be resolved quickly.

The following morning, I received a call from a Houston police officer who told me that Carolyn had been moved to LBJ Hospital for the treatment of lupus (she had been taking a prescription medication for lupus-like symptoms). The officer went on to tell me that we would not be allowed to visit her at the hospital.

I called Marilyn, who had spent the night with her mother, to tell her what I had just learned about Carolyn. We talked briefly, through a thinly veiled sadness, about what we should do to help her. Since she had not been living with us, we were not sure of all that had been going on in her life. Against the uncertainty we faced, we looked forward to having Van with us.

On the morning of the third day, I accepted another collect telephone call from Carolyn. She told me that she had been released from the hospital and was back in a holding tank at the jail. Her voice faltered and her crying broke my heart. "The pain," she said, "is awful." Then, I heard her say, "I'm going to die." Although I did not believe she was near death, it was not hard to understand that she felt like dying. I told her that her mother and I loved her just before the line went dead. Then, I called the jail to ask if we could visit Carolyn. The deputy explained that she would not be allowed to have visitors until "classification" determined where she would be located inside the jail. I asked, "When will that happen?" "Maybe tomorrow," he answered. I had never visited anyone in jail and knew nothing about jail visitation.

I continued to call the jail with questions about visitation but I felt as if the answers to those questions were not provided with a spirit of genuine helpfulness. Later that same day, I picked up Van at Houston's William P. Hobby Airport and told him the bad news about his sister. He was surprised and deeply saddened. After arriving back home, Van talked to his mother on the telephone. Then, he and I made plans to go together the next day to visit Carolyn. It was a time when our world of safety and security was about to be tested and the troublesome aspect of lost control was about to surface. Against the uneasiness and uncertainty of what we faced regarding Carolyn's trouble, I concluded that prayer was the most reliable resource available to us. These words from the prayer hymn by Henry F. Lyte are a strong resource for times of trouble:

> When other helpers fail and comforts flee,
> Help of the helpless, O abide with me.

We left the car in a parking lot on Franklin Street just across from the massive twelve-story jail. After entering the building, an employee of the county directed us to a large loose-leaf binder located on a table near where the visitation line was forming. We were told that it contained the names, identification numbers, and the building location of every inmate in the jail. Quickly turning the pages, it didn't take us long to find the information needed in order to prepare ourselves for what came next.

When we reached the head of the waiting line, a deputy asked to see our driver's licenses. He then handed me a small form to be filled out with our names, as visitors, and Carolyn's name, as the inmate to be visited, along with her inmate number and the place she was located. We walked through a metal detector without having a warning issued against either of us and stepped into an elevator that took us to our twelfth-floor destination.

I slipped the information form that I held in my hand under the window of the control station and watched as a deputy picked it up. Van and I sat down in chairs facing a broad window through which we could see the large room where jail inmates came for their visits and where they were seated on metal stools firmly attached to the floor. A jailer sat at a desk inside the room keeping track of the time of each visit.

We hadn't waited long when Carolyn came through the door into the visitation room. The bright orange jail clothing she wore contrasted sharply with the paleness of her face. She appeared tired but there was no doubt how glad she was to see us. Words were exchanged hesitantly as Van and I took turns talking to Carolyn through the Plexiglas barrier. Her soft voice became lost to us at times within the loud verbal exchanges of those in whose company we found ourselves. We did hear her say that she had been given Motrin for her joint pain and was feeling a little better.

After completing our brief twenty-minute visit, we took the elevator back downstairs where I decided I would ask if we could see the chaplain. We lined up at a window where it seemed as if we might obtain some information. Before long we were staring into the face of a stern looking deputy. When I asked about seeing the chaplain, he replied, "The chaplains are all busy." When I asked about getting books to my daughter, he said, "They have plenty of reading material." At that point, a man who was standing in line behind us overheard our conversation and told us that we could copy pages of books and mail them to the inmate at the jail address. I would not forget how much this simple act of kindness from a stranger, one who was no doubt experienced in supporting a loved one in jail, meant to us at a moment of such inner turmoil.

After depositing some cash in an inmate trust fund for Carolyn, Van and I walked away from the jail, saying very little, each of us thinking about the trouble that had come upon us. Later, a thought entered my mind concerning the men and women occupying jail cells: Jesus pleads for them. I was shaken by the implications of such divine love for all who have gone astray.

Marilyn went with me to visit Carolyn the next day. I was relieved by how calmly she talked with our daughter through the glass barrier. Carolyn answered all of her mother's questions about daily living inside the jail. The nature of the conversation helped to take away a few of the upsetting thoughts we had about such an alien environment and, at the same time, seemed to relieve Carolyn of having to go into detail regarding the criminal charges that would be filed against her. As a result, our visit enabled us to tell her, with spontaneous simplicity, how much we loved her.

When Carolyn first entered the jail, I was unprepared to accept the worst that could happen to her within the criminal justice system. I thought that it would only be a matter of days before something would happen to turn things around for her. As I called to mind all that Carolyn had done for others, along with her good work record, my illusions of her imminent rescue expanded.

I remember offering a prayer that Carolyn might accept the terms of God's conditional promise (as I imagined it might come to her): "From there (from jail and prison) you will seek the Lord your God and you will find him if you search after him will all your heart and soul" (Deut 4:29). As it turned out, such hope was fulfilled but not within the short period of time that I expected.

WILDERNESS CHALLENGES

Marilynne Robinson, in her wonderful novel *Gilead*, has the Rev. John Ames thinking about his upcoming sermon on Genesis 21:14–21, the story of Hagar and Ishmael. The thought comes to him, through prayer, that God's provisions made it possible for Ishmael, son of Abraham and Hagar, to survive the wilderness.

> That is how life goes—we send our children into the wilderness. Some of them on the day they are born, it seems, for all the help

we can give them. Some of them seem to be a kind of wilderness unto themselves. But there must be angels there, too, and springs of water. Even that wilderness, the very habitation of jackals, is the Lord's. I need to bear this in mind.[1]

Scriptural allusions to the wilderness as a place of danger and desolation are appropriate to jails and prisons. As I sought ways to deflect the shock and sadness of this wilderness claim on our lives, I went to the Psalms and immediately identified with the psalmist who cried out in despair, "I am poured out like water, and all my bones are out of joint" (Ps 22:14). During the hardest times, I used the psalmist's words to beseech God: "But you, O Lord, do not be far away! O my help, come quickly to my aid" (Ps 22:19). A short time later, I found in Walter Brueggemann's work on the Psalms the promise of a hope that exists within the very trouble from which I prayed that we might be delivered. The guidance I received from this scholar of critical learning helped me to recognize my impulse of control. This allowed me to embrace the expansiveness of God's love and mercy as a part of being faithful in a world where the painful issues of life are not easily resolved. As opposed to the psalmist's boastful assertion, "the Lord has rewarded me according to my righteousness; according to the cleanliness of my hands, he recompensed me" (Ps 18:20), I repeated to myself the words of the hymn, "In my hand no price I bring; simply to thy cross I cling."[2]

Those who pass through the portals of a jail for the first time to visit a loved one being held on a criminal charge are generally unaware of the wilderness implications of what they are facing. While keeping the news to themselves, many of them entertain hopes that their loved one will be found innocent or, after all the evidence has been obtained, that the crime will turn out to be less serious than the initial charge reflects.

Families who have gone through previous wilderness experiences with a loved one are not as likely to be surprised when yet another call is received from the police station or jail. Some angrily declare they have had enough and are "washing their hands" of any further responsibility. Others wearily continue their support in spite of repeated instances of troublesome behavior. Many never reach a point where a song of deliverance can be sung.

---

1. Robinson, *Gilead*, 119. Copyright © 2004 Marilynne Robinson. Reprinted by permission of Farrar, Straus and Giroux, LLC.

2. From the hymn, "Rock of Ages," written by Augustus M. Toplady.

There are times when a family may feel as if there are healing possibilities within the wilderness. They cling to the hope that if their loved one is locked up for awhile it might help to bring about some positive life changes. For example, I heard a father say, concerning his daughter's relatively short sentence, "Maybe this will knock some sense into her." However, some of those who entertain this thought are shocked when they realize how many negative things can happen in jail, such as being attacked by another inmate or failing to receive needed prescription medication. Jail confinement also holds the potential for causing severe depression.

The parents of a son or daughter in jail may not, in their self-preoccupation, be able to cope with the bewilderment that such trouble presents to them. Disappointed, hurt, and confused, they become immobilized, saying and doing little, and dwelling on their hurt too privately. They are likely to come up with unrealistic arguments supporting the innocence of the one they brought into the world. Some, it seems, never come to terms with the truth that their loved one has committed a crime. Or, their thinking never goes beyond the rationalization that what happened was the fault of someone else.

Family members who are angry with a loved one jailed on a criminal charge seem, at times, to be part of the wilderness. From time to time, they can be heard in visitation lines and during visits heaping condemnation upon sons and daughters for causing them shame and disgrace. We wondered about ways through which parents may contribute to bringing a loved one down.

The decision to offer support to a loved one through the wilderness of jail time should not be dependent upon the presumption that he or she is innocent of criminal charges. Many family members are inclined to be too trusting. After boldly asserting their confidence in defense attorneys who have convinced them that acquittal is a "slam dunk," some families never seem able to accept the fact that their loved one is going to prison.

The jail, no matter what wilderness trials and tribulations it presents, is under God. And, in the seemingly random manner through which anything good happens in the jail, there are signs of God's provisions for those who have eyes to see and ears to hear.

THE JAIL EXPERIENCE

Noise, confusion, and discomfort greet new arrivals to the crowded quarters of many county jails. Before anything else happens, these new inmates are placed in a large room, often called a "holding tank," and allowed to make one telephone call. Privacy is not respected as body orifices are checked and a medicinal shower is often administered to eliminate lice. The clothing and all personal possessions of the accused men and women are confiscated and marked as "property" that can be picked up later by a family member or someone else designated by the jailed suspect.

The procedures for booking include obtaining fingerprints and taking a picture of the accused. The picture, called a "mug shot," is guaranteed to be the worst picture for which the new jail tenant has ever posed. Jail clothing is issued along with a few necessities such as a toothbrush and tooth powder. In most instances, a perfunctory physical exam is conducted along with an interview to obtain information necessary for the records. Some county jails give handbooks to new inmates that contain information about jail procedures, including how to file a grievance.

A new jail occupant is given an identification number, a location (cell block or individual cell), case number, court number, judge's name, charge, bond amount, and a court date. Protective custody is afforded to those who might be exposed to danger in a heavily occupied cell block because of a high profile, inflammatory, or controversial case.

Family members and visitors are not allowed to bring stamps, toiletry items, or snacks to inmates. These items may only be purchased at the commissary with funds deposited in an inmate trust fund. Visitors may not personally bring mail or reading material to an inmate. In most situations, books and other published material can be mailed to the inmate directly from a publisher or recognized bookstore. Some jails will allow writing material from a recognized office supply store to be mailed to an inmate. These are examples of rules established by the jails in order to maintain the strictest form of security.

The medical needs of a loved one in jail, such as dietary requirements and prescription drugs, must have a physician's order. Bringing special food or prescribed drugs into the jail from the outside is specifically forbidden. The family should be prepared to wait for days before any of these needs are substantiated and acted upon by the jail medical staff. In addition, family members should keep notes of conversations with medical personnel associated with the jail, being sure to include dates and names. These notes may need to be shared with other family members or friends who are involved as caregivers.

The questions family members normally ask when a loved one may be facing time in prison are about what was done, why it was done, and who else was involved. They may find it hard, at first, to piece together what really happened. The explanations they are given may not include all the facts. There may be extenuating circumstances including the role of an accomplice. The use of drugs or alcohol is often a factor. The claim of innocence is frequently offered. To make matters more confusing, families sometimes receive information from other sources that either diminish or exaggerate the seriousness of the crime.

Each person who has been arrested on a criminal charge is informed of his or her constitutional rights during the first appearance before a judge. At this time, there will be a formal charge or, in case of insufficient evidence, a release. If there is a formal charge, bail will be set if it has not been set earlier. Those who are tried and found guilty will remain in the county jail an undetermined amount of time before being taken to a state facility.

BAIL

We became aware of the large number of bonding companies located close to the Harris County Jail after we started visiting Carolyn. Many of them feature neon lighting in order to attract nighttime customers. These businesses, hardly noticed by those who remain free of what keeps them operating, exude tragedy. They are the setting for transactions involving those whose earnest desire is to spare loved ones from time in jail by "bonding them out." As such, their operation is one essentially designed to profit from crime.

Bail is a security amount set by the court and posted by the defendant or someone acting on behalf of the defendant. Those who put up a bond for the accused do so in good faith, counting on their friend or loved one to appear before the proper court at the scheduled time to answer the charges brought against him or her. The amount of bail is set in accordance with the facts known about the case. They include seriousness of the crime, previous criminal record, the likelihood of flight from the state, and the possibility of committing new offenses while on bond. In some cases, bail is denied.

Family members should be cautious in bailing a loved one out too quickly. Careful consideration should be given to their loved one's prior pattern of behavior and what might be best under the circumstances before deciding to commit personal resources to making a bond. This decision is crucial because if an inmate is out on bond and does not appear in the proper court on the proper date and time, the bond is forfeited. This leads, all too often, to losing life savings and home equities. What is more, it can bring about the feeling of a trust betrayed.

JAIL VISITATION ORIENTATION

Jail confinement is the first penalty that must be paid for being charged with a crime. As a result, jails are places where anxiousness over what the future will hold captures the mind and spirit of everyone closely connected to the accused. Family members who have no idea what their loved one has done to get there approach jails with fear and uncertainty. The jails do not offer orientation classes for first-time visitors and what is learned about visitation through telephone conversations with jail employees is limited. Some restrictions regarding visitation may not be mentioned and those who are expecting otherwise may not learn until they arrive that physical contact with their loved one is not allowed.

The first visit is filled with mixed emotions. There are feelings of alienation and regret that alternate with feelings of sympathy and sadness. As the visitation area is approached, questions come to mind, such as: What should I say? What questions should I ask? What should not be said or asked? In the midst of such emotional upheaval, remembering to pray is important.

Visitors and inmates are separated by a Plexiglas barrier, which further complicates communication in a setting that is already very noisy. Some of these barriers have small holes drilled into a central portion of the Plexiglas and covered by a round louvered shield. Others have strips of heavy mesh tightly connected just under the Plexiglas through which the conversation is channeled. We found the best communication procedure to be a telephone hook-up. The use of phones helps to minimize the noise and, where two phone extensions are available on the outside, a three-person conversation can be conducted.

HELP FOR A DAY OF TROUBLE

Call on me in the day of trouble;
I will deliver you and you shall glorify me.

—Psalm 50:15

One Sunday morning, during the first days of sadness and confusion over Carolyn's arrest on criminal charges, we entered the church and came face to face with our pastor, Jim Moore. He asked, "How are you doing?" Marilyn answered, "We are here," to which he replied, "This is where you should be."

On our visits to the jail, we overheard many expressions of sadness, frustration, and anger over jail conditions. In the midst of our own vexations, the thought came to me of how music is able to convey a special kind of peace. I became attentive to anthems, litanies, and hymns that speak to the pain of loss and alienation. Thomas Moore's hymn, "Come, Ye Disconsolate," is just such a hymn.

> Come ye disconsolate, where'er ye languish
> Come to the mercy seat, fervently kneel.
> Here bring your wounded hearts, here tell your anguish:
> Earth has no sorrow that heaven cannot heal.

We did not decide right away what to do about obtaining legal assistance for Carolyn. An attorney who I tentatively engaged to advise us offered the somewhat encouraging assessment that what Carolyn was facing was "a classic case of duress." Not long afterward, Marilyn and I attended a pretrial hearing where, seated near the back of the courtroom, we were unable to hear the conversation that took place between the attorney representing Carolyn and the judge. After the session ended, the attorney came over to where we were standing. He had a worried and somewhat incredulous look on his face. He said, "They are talking about prison time!" I became convinced at that moment that we were not standing on a firm legal foundation.

When I realized the potential seriousness of the charges Carolyn faced, I decided to call an attorney friend, Robins Brice, who served on the Holly Hall Board of Directors. We met for lunch and I told him the story of Carolyn's situation. He got up from the table where we were eating and called a criminal law attorney with whom he was acquainted. The attorney's name was Bill Burge and he happened, at that particular time, to be free. Robins accompanied me to his downtown office.

I received from Bill Burge a candid evaluation of the charges against Carolyn. In spite of my hopes being dashed, I appreciated such a frank assessment of the situation we faced. I talked with Marilyn, who had become regularly occupied with caring for her mother. She advised me to do whatever I thought best. I decided that if the prosecutor was talking about prison time, we needed a respected and competent attorney to represent Carolyn.

Bill proved to be a powerful advocate for Carolyn. Popular depictions of the advocacy provided by defense attorneys often show them swaying jurors with provocative testimony and theatrical closing statements. A far more important dimension of advocacy requires the defense attorney to correctly read the political and legal landscape in order to provide the client with a realistic picture of their prospects within the legal system. Bill painted a vivid picture of Carolyn's prospects in a mock cross-examination where he played the role of prosecutor with Carolyn on the stand. This proved to be a harsh but necessary exercise that clarified the decisions Carolyn needed to make.

Bill understood that Harris County juries tended to dispense "justice" with long prison sentences. However, he felt that if Carolyn would be willing to cooperate with the prosecutor, an agreement could be reached where "justice" in Harris County would be tempered with a small degree of mercy. The agreement that Carolyn signed was not an indictment of others but rather an explanation and acceptance of responsibility for her role in what had transpired. In exchange for signing this agreement, Carolyn received a prison sentence of ten years.

We were convinced that Carolyn, in following the advice of her attorney, was provided with the best possible solution to the charges she faced. As a result, we could concentrate on helping her through the time she would have to spend in prison as a preparation for bringing her home. Prayer did not locate Bill Burge, but prayer located us in the sanctuary of God's love and mercy where one good thing or another happens to cause rejoicing even in sorrow. Here are some suggestions for those whose experience of a loved one's incarceration is just beginning and who will need the kind of direction that will lead them through a time of confusion and uncertainty.

1. Avoid anger and condemnation while visiting with your loved one. Let your love be expressed freely without assuming anything about the criminal charges.

2. Educate yourself about what is being faced by your loved one by obtaining legal advice from a reliable source.

3. Offer thanks to God for every gift of understanding that brings relief from fear or anxiety. Share what you are facing with a trusted minister or friend.

4. Ask God's forgiveness for the ways you may have failed to do the right thing for your loved one and seek to clear up any misunderstandings that may exist between you and others who care for your loved one.

5. Let music speak to your sadness or regret. Stay connected to the psalmists and to faithful song-makers whose music brings healing to hurting hearts.

2

Jail Time

Not surprisingly, criminologists have described jails as the 'strange social hybrids' of the correctional landscape, as 'detention centers for suspects.' They have been called the 'poorhouses of the twentieth century,' the 'ultimate ghettos,' the 'social garbage cans' used to discard 'society's rabble.'[1]

—Jennifer Wynn

JAILS AND PRISONS SERVE different purposes. Jails impact the lives of the largest number of people nationwide. They contain men and women who have been arrested on criminal charges prior to their cases being heard and their guilt or innocence determined. A large number of those who are found guilty of misdemeanor offenses will complete their sentences in the county jail. Others who receive a guilty verdict on a felony charge will stay in the jail only until they are assigned to a state prison. The largest number of men and women who occupy space in the Harris County Jail in Houston, Texas, (with a total capacity of around 10,000) is made up of those who have been charged with a crime and who are waiting for their cases to be heard.

WHO ARE THESE PEOPLE?

First-time jail occupants may look around and say, "Who are these people?" The implication, of course, is that "these people" are not like the people they are used to being around. Many others who wait in jail for something to move their cases forward will see people they know or have run into on the streets. They will understand the language being spoken and will not be surprised by the volume of noise. In heavily populated city

1. Wynn, *Inside Rikers*, 6.

jails they form one large polyphonic mass of humanity, a multi-ethnic mix coming mostly from burdened inner city communities. And, always, there are those who appear as if they do not belong, offering the sad testimony that crime knows no boundaries. There are lonely people, at odds with the world, who seem strangely at home within the impersonal custody of the jail. There are other individuals whose faces mirror shame, their eyes searching anxiously for some way out. And, always, within the jail, there are those who plaintively ask, "Who am I and what am I doing here?"

There are some first-time offenders who are distraught over having done something so bad that it has put them in the company of "criminals." Others are only sorry they were caught. Some actually seem confused about why charges were filed against them in the first place. Unwilling to admit their guilt, they repeatedly gloss over the seriousness of their criminal actions by offering the explanation: "I was at the wrong place at the wrong time." Then, there are the drifters, the ones who move between pretense and possibility and are always being pushed one way or the other, in and out of jail, almost recovered—but never completely.

In addition to those who commit crimes of violence, countless numbers are in jail having been caught dealing drugs. People who live "in the streets," many of whom are mentally disturbed, are known to commit petty crimes in order to survive and end up in jail where they have food to eat and a place to sleep. Individuals who exhibit psychotic behavior and try to hurt imagined tormentors often end up in jail. Those who are taken into jail custody who pose a serious threat to themselves are put on suicide watch and placed inside a closely monitored private cell.

Many jail inmates, like the psalmists, think a lot about enemies. There are so many people to blame for their trouble: "If this person had not gotten in my way . . . ," "If I had not been threatened . . . ," "If she had not spent all of my weekly wages . . . ," "If that cop had only followed his normal routine . . . ," "If there had not been the choking incident . . . ," "If my father had not beaten me up so often . . . ," "If the dealer had not set me up. . . ." Enemies are everywhere and can be anyone. Family members may hear threats of revenge against someone else being held in the jail, someone their loved one is blaming for the circumstances they both now face.

When substance abuse offenses were increasing dramatically several years ago, broadly interpreted sentencing guidelines created a new category of jail inmates. While backgrounds of wealth and privilege keep some of these violators out of jail, or enable them to manage limited time sentences, there are others whose repeated drug cases, along with more serious criminal actions in conjunction with them, place them beyond any hope of obtaining a quick release.

There are more than a few individuals who feel a sense of relief when they are first apprehended by law enforcement authorities. Drug use and the stupor brought about by various mind-altering substances, along with sleeplessness, leaves them exhausted and totally nonresistant to arrest. No matter what they have done, and without condoning their actions, there is a time to accept the sad consequences of those who have done wrong and to actively support their recovery.

HOW CAN WE LIVE HERE?

Our transgressions and our sins weigh upon us,
and we waste away because of them; how then can we live?

—Ezekiel 33:10b

Those who find themselves in jail for the first time are properly advised against the kind of behavior that would call attention to themselves. They should take to heart the advice "to not see anything but, at the same time, to be aware of everything." When these new jail tenants receive a location assignment, they should not be surprised or hesitant when seasoned inmate greeters ask the question, "Who you gonna ride with?" The best response to that question is: "I came in alone and I'm leaving alone." If they are challenged to fight, they should do so only in self-defense. Unfortunately, the weakest inmates are in the greatest danger and very seldom will anyone step forward in their defense.

While Carolyn was in the Harris County Jail, Marilyn selected Natalie Sleeth's "Hymn of Promise" as a spiritual theme for Carolyn's life. Marilyn mailed a copy of the hymn to Carolyn and one morning when we received her call from the jail, I held the telephone so that she could hear her mother play it on the piano. This special note of joy, linking words and music, gave Carolyn an important lift for facing the day.

Marilyn and I expressed our love for Carolyn through regular visits, a wide assortment of mailings, and a modest amount of cash credited to her commissary account. Her brother, Van, visited her at every opportunity when he was home from his studies at Kansas University. Carolyn also received visits from two minister friends, Ron Morris from St Luke's United Methodist Church, and Terry Thompson from St. Paul's United Methodist Church. The two of them helped to ease the weight of her transgressions through their gift of conversation and prayer.

In response to the question, "How can I possibly make it here?" Carolyn decided to start writing about her experiences. She imagined herself on special assignment and, as a consequence, committed her time to recording what she saw and heard. She thought about how such writing might serve as a warning to others of the importance of avoiding ever having to be in such a place. She wishes to make clear, however, that nothing she writes is meant to blame anyone or any system for the conditions through which she lived. Her intent is simply to describe the conditions, as well as some of the people in jail with her, from the perspective of her confinement within the borders of a strange land.

THE HARRIS COUNTY JAIL

I remember the cold showers in Section 12B5 in the Harris County Jail. I cringe when I think of the discomfort of showering in icy water. I remember the disgust I felt in the shower in Block 1104 as I watched the large cockroaches crawl in and out of the drain around my feet. And, just as the temperature can be too cold, it also can be too hot. I remember my red skin after the occasional scalding shower. On some occasions a deputy will actually enter the "tank" and make rounds in between count time. This does not happen often but when it does inmates in the day area automatically shout a kind of warning to other inmates who are in their cells. One day the exchange went something like this when the gates opened and the deputy walked in:

Inmate: 'Police in the house!'

Deputy: 'Now what's going on in here that you have to warn everyone that I'm in here.

Inmate: 'Nothing's going on but wouldn't you want to be warned if one of *us* was in *your* house?'

A 'new house' (inmate) who obviously knew nothing about jail had the following exchange with the jailer on duty:

Inmate: 'What time does court start, I need to go to court this morning?'

Jailer: 'Do you have a watch?'

Inmate: 'No.'

Jailer: 'Do you have a key?'

Inmate: 'No, I just have to go to court.'

Jailer: 'Let me tell you something. You left your right to tell time, your right to choose, and your right to decide at the door when you were booked into this high-rise. If the system decides you are to be in court, me or another representative of the system will come take your sorry ____ there at the time the system decides for you to be there. Any Questions?'

Inmate: 'Do you have any blow dryers here?' (Many remain clueless.)

PAM OR THE PRINCE OF DARKNESS?

We were saddened to hear stories from inside the jail that pointed, in different ways, to the ongoing tragedy of those whose lives are burdened by hopelessness. One day, in a letter from the Harris County Jail, Carolyn described a chaplain's routine visit in a cell block of women inmates.

The chaplain came around and asked: 'Has everyone been able to get along this week?'

Inmate's reply: 'We had a bad week, chaplain.'

The chaplain asked, 'Why, what happened?'

The inmate explained: 'Well, there was a big fight and this girl got moved; her name was Pam and she threatened to cut everybody.'

The chaplain answered: 'You have to remember, when something like that happens; it wasn't Pam, it was the Prince of Darkness,' to which the offender replied, 'I don't know, chaplain, it sure as hell looked like Pam.'

The question, "Was it Pam or was it Prince of Darkness?" has broad implications. Was it Pam whose poor choices as an individual resulted in arrest, conviction, and jail time? Or was it the conditions surrounding her life from infancy, conditions fostered by what Paul spoke of in his letter to the church at Ephesus as the "principalities and powers and world rulers of this present darkness?" (Eph 6:12).

Martin Luther's hymn, "A Mighty Fortress is our God," refers to the Prince of Darkness as one whose "rage we can endure." However, it is hard for the masses living in neighborhoods infested with crime, disease, substance abuse, and an absence of love to endure the rage. Many in these areas do not have the resources to keep people from being controlled by unresolved anger, bitter resentment against authority, and finally, criminal activity.

After several months in the Harris County Jail, Carolyn served shorter periods of time in other county jails. First, she was required to answer a bench warrant from Tarrant County. Second, there was one charge from Galveston County that needed to be accepted as part of the Harris County agreement. When we first became aware of the movement of offenders across the state, we heard the words "pulling a chain" to describe it. Sometimes called simply a "chain," this expression is likely to have come from earlier days when inmates were chained together outside jails or from the work gangs that pulled chains through their field labor.

ONE NIGHT IN THE JEFFERSON COUNTY JAIL

The transporting of offenders from one location to another often takes many twists and turns. Instead of heading out from Houston on Highway 45 and arriving at the Ft. Worth destination within a few hours, they took Carolyn the long way—through Beaumont—where she spent one night in the Jefferson County Jail.

> I was deposited in a holdover cell for one person and the best way I can describe it is to compare it with a telephone booth with a toilet crammed inside. There was a little window in the door of my cell through which I had a perfect view of a clock upon which my gaze remained constant for the majority of the night, that is, between prayers. At approximately two o'cock a.m., the door to the cell opened and to my surprise, Shelly was placed into this cell with me. It was a cell clearly designed to be occupied by only one person. I could no longer lie down so we sat side by side in that phone booth sized cell for the duration of the night. Evidently, Shelly had been harassed in the cell where she was before and that was what brought about her move. I can't forget the fact that the toilet did not flush which made things a bit more unpleasant. At 5:00 a.m., the cell door opened once again and two breakfast trays were somehow squeezed inside. Shelly ate what was on both trays. As I drank the milk, I remember wondering how anyone could possibly have an appetite under those circumstances.

THE TARRANT COUNTY JAIL

Carolyn's next stop was on West Belknap Street in downtown Ft. Worth. This was where, in a holding tank full of inmates, she made her first telephone call to us from the Tarrant County Jail. There was only one commode and one sink to serve the needs of everyone in the open tank. A call the next day revealed to us that she had been assigned a cell on the medical floor as a result of her various health problems. The inmates on this floor were allowed only one hour outside of their cells every twenty-four hours.

When Marilyn and I visited Carolyn the following Saturday, having driven the 288 miles from Houston to Ft. Worth, we were allowed a forty-five minute visit because of the travel distance. We were surprised by how different the visitation procedure was from Harris County. After being checked in, we were directed to an elevator that took us to the fifth floor. The small visitation area we entered contained only eight stools, all facing the Plexiglas barrier. When Carolyn opened the door into the inmate area opposite to where we were seated and smoke trailed in after her, we received ample proof that smoking was a common practice on the fifth floor.

Marilyn and I spent the night in Ft. Worth where I had a hard time going to sleep. As I worried long into the night over what Carolyn was enduring, the words of Charles Wesley's hymn, "Jesus, Lover of My Soul," entered my mind. I kept repeating the familiar words, "Cover my defenseless head with the shadow of thy wing," until sleep finally overcame my despair. The next morning, we attended the Sunday worship service of the Meadowbrook United Methodist Church where Gary Whitbeck served as pastor. Gary had already been to see Carolyn at the jail following a call he received from Bishop Joe Wilson's secretary with whom I had visited about Carolyn. The greeting we received from Gary just before the service started was uplifting. The repeated theme of his pastoral prayer, as well as his message, revolved around the frequently repeated words, "Oh, how we need a savior." As the result of such spiritual strengthening, we were better prepared for our visit with Carolyn that afternoon. The following two Saturdays, I took a flight to Dallas, rented a car, and drove to Ft. Worth to visit Carolyn. At the beginning of both of these visits I tried unsuccessfully to get the jail authorities to accept a packet of Benadryl for Carolyn to use for her allergy problem. Her difficulty in breathing was aggravated by the cigarette smoke that permeated the entire area where she was confined. Carolyn wrote from her cell in the Tarrant County Jail:

> The filth of the shower at the Tarrant County Jail is so far unmatched. The roaches, the slime, and the smell make it difficult to experience a shower as cleansing. Also, the button has to be held down constantly or the water will not stay on. It is hard work taking a shower. The shower 'curtain' is actually a clear garbage bag and the showerhead is actually a plastic shampoo bottle with the bottom cut out of it.

Another mailing contained this sad story:

> The day started early for Diane and, therefore, for the rest of us as well. Shortly after breakfast, around five a.m., a brutal struggle took place in Diane's cell. She was fighting with her mattress and cursing it violently. She was throwing the mattress around in her cell as if it was her worst enemy. She was blaming the person represented by the mattress for stealing her welfare check and her wrath was apparent. She was out of breath by the time the 'fight' ended. Later, during that same day, I heard water being sloshed around in Diane's cell and I became curious. The answer I received, as I later walked by Diane's cell, was somewhat unsettling. There was Diane, seated comfortably on the floor in front of the toilet looking surprisingly content as she washed her socks in the toilet just as if it was a basin specifically designed for such a purpose.

The conditions described in Carolyn's writing from within the Tarrant County Jail caused me to label them, "The Horrors of West Belknap Street." We were told about a horrid "de-bugging" ritual designed to get rid of lice and the late night screams from an inmate who, after a lengthy delay, was finally taken away to where she suffered a miscarriage. There were emaciated AIDS victims and prostitutes. There were wild cries coupled with the sobbing and laughter of madness from the seriously demented whose lives drugs had ruined.

Carolyn wrote to us a frank assessment of the situation she faced in her confinement.

> I don't want to ever fit in with this crowd but I am here. Unfortunately, my actions have gained me admission to this section of society. I want *out*. I don't want to be one of 'them.' But it is too late. I can't change what happened, I can only control what I do with the experience. I contemplate constantly how I can change

such a negative situation into a positive outcome. I haven't figured that one out yet. I have plenty of time if I can only survive. It is not the aspect of confinement *per se* that brings me down. I am resigned fully to the fact that I have time to serve. The difficult part is with the facts of life that accompany this confinement: The filth, the insanity, the bugs, the lack of edible food, etc. I believe I will eventually be able to settle into a workable routine and reach a place where I will be able to do something nourishing. I believe I will reach a place where the roaches do not crawl from the ceiling to the floor all the time. I believe it will be in a place where 'bug showers' are not necessary and where all of the other occupants are not dying or insane. I believe it will be a place where I do not have to make the choice of lighting cigarettes or being spit upon. I have trust that I will arrive at such a place.

The news of Carolyn's unexpected move to a different location within the Tarrant County jail offered us some encouragement. There was one especially positive aspect. There was a tiny window next to her top bunk through which she could see the sky.

A woman called "Mother Mary" was the acknowledged leader of the group in the new location. As a recent convert to Christianity she, in seeking ways to witness to the others, immediately saw something different about Carolyn. One day, Mother Mary noticed Carolyn's neat writing and asked her if she would print some passages of scripture on pieces of paper to hand out to the others. Because of how much alike she printed each page, she earned the nickname, "Miss Xerox." For a brief period, the cell block had a human copy machine, strangely in line with the monks of old who, in their cells, made copies of the sacred texts. Sentence messages from the Bible, in a terrible place of human habitation, were placed into waiting hands. In Cell Block 25B, the copy work became a faithful service. We were touched by the thought of a jail inmate, one so special to us, being a scribe of the Lord.

AN UNEXPECTED RETURN
TO THE HARRIS COUNTY JAIL

Carolyn's bench warrant was finally cleared and the next morning she was told to get her things together. Before loading her into the transportation van, they put shackles around her ankles and chained her wrists together behind her back. The cramped ride south from Ft. Worth involved an unusual stop along the way. Inexperienced escorts took several of their chained passengers into an Exxon station store where customers gasped in amazement. As the day wore on, one of the inmates was dropped off at the state jail near Dayton, Texas. Finally, after making a wrong turn, the driver got lost and asked the ones remaining on board if any of them could tell her which way to go in order to reach their next delivery point in downtown Houston.

Marilyn and I were surprised when we received a telephone call from Carolyn telling us that she was back in Houston at the Harris County Jail. The intake people, she said, were uncertain over what to do with her since Harris County no longer had jurisdiction over her. A letter I had received from a captain in the Sheriff's Department stated that Carolyn would be taken directly from Ft. Worth to Galveston. I found it interesting that he closed his letter by inviting me to call him if he could be of any further assistance.

The Harris County Sheriff's Department did not know what to do with Carolyn, dropped unexpectedly at their door. They ended up booking her on the original charges and placing her in the same protective custody cell on the twelfth floor that she occupied before. There, she received a friendly welcome from several of the inmates who were there when she left for Ft. Worth. I called the captain, with his letter in my hand, to ask what had happened. He explained that a mistake had been made and that it would be corrected in a few weeks.

One morning, about ten days after Carolyn arrived back in Houston from Ft. Worth, one of the inmates from the cell block where she was located called to say that Carolyn had been taken away. Marilyn and I were positive that she would be waiting for her next visit somewhere within the Galveston County Jail.

THE GALVESTON COUNTY JAIL

The Galveston County Jail was different from the others in a number of ways. The area we entered to be processed for our visit had a large picture window looking out across a boat dock. When we arrived, we were given a number and told to wait until we were called. To get to the tiny visitation "cubby hole" that accommodated Pod J visitors, Marilyn and I passed through a monitored doorway and a maze of doors, corridors, and stairs. One aspect of visitation at this location that we will not forget was the heavy, crashing sound of doors closing that reverberated down the hallways. Carolyn wrote us letters describing the living conditions in Pod J of the Galveston County Jail, telling how it was for her to be confined to one large room with twenty-five to thirty other inmates while being watched over by one female deputy.

Aside from the constant noise and chaos, it has simply been too cold to do much of anything, such as thinking and writing. I have experienced being cold many times before in my life but there is something different about being cold in jail. It reminds me of another aspect of life that I no longer have control over. Being cold in jail cannot be resolved by simply putting on a coat or extra clothes. It is not a matter of adjusting a thermostat—this is an environment where the climate is controlled. The only ones allowed to regulate the thermostat are the jail maintenance personnel. We bear some semblance to lizards in our green suits, crawling around each other, appearing much like useless creatures as we go through the motions of existence. I think of Mom as I wash my t-shirt, underwear, and socks by hand in the tiny sink attached to the metal toilet. There is no other way. I think of Mom checking the tags of my clothes to see if they were machine washable. I will be washing by hand for a long time now. When I think of the times I got angry with Mom for washing my clothes for me I feel ashamed. Norene is in the bunk next to mine. She took the liberty of showing me a loose razor blade that she had hidden in the frame of her bunk. She said that it's 'just in case she has to cut somebody up in here.' Not a comforting thought. It makes the contraband searches seem that much more ridiculous. If someone wants something in jail they can get it. It's just a matter of finding the right supply source. The 'weekend warrior' comes in on Friday evening and leaves on Sunday evening. She claims that this 'sentence' fits her schedule perfectly and allows her to party all week and then come into jail long enough to rest up. Each time she comes she is faithful to bring with her a generous supply of powder cocaine for her buddies in jail. The saying around her is: 'If you're a woman you have a built-in suitcase.' The idea is disgusting but it is put into play quite often in jail. Of course, precautions are taken against this when we have to 'squat and cough' during a strip search, but as with anything else, there are ways around the system.

Clara is a woman 59 years of age who is in jail on suspicion of theft. One of the other inmates asked for her address in the 'world' so they could correspond after they each leave jail. Clara replied that she doesn't have an address out in the 'world.' She added that the only time she can claim to have an address is when she is in jail. Fay says that she has been to prison four times and that she cries every time she has to leave. Tragic! Katy is an alcoholic and a cocaine addict. She claims that she wants to stop coming to jail but she admits that she will not stop drinking. She said she will not stop until she kills someone and then she will come back to stay.

I am trying to get a grasp on understanding the people who surround me. One minute they pray out loud for each other and the next minute curses fly between them like hailstones. One minute they pray out loud for the justice system to be lenient on them and the next minute they laugh loudly and mock the system that governs them. I have watched women laugh with each other, watch TV with each other, and even pray with each other, and then, when the other is not looking or is in the shower, I have watched them steal from each other. There is no honor among thieves. Nothing is sacred. They ask each other, 'What's the first thing you are going to do when you get out of this place?' The answer: 'Buy a rock.' Others boast that someone will have a 'rock' waiting for them when they get out. These are people who have been brought in for the possession of crack cocaine. For them, jail is a place where you can get meals, some rest, and medical care if it is needed, and then go back out to resume the assault on their own bodies with crack being the weapon. This group of people seems to live in more deprivation outside of jail, except for the availability of the drugs. Jail, then, actually encourages the cycle of addiction. One woman states that after she has been in jail for weeks she actually feels like going to the mall on a rampage of 'boosting' (shoplifting). The women laugh at the methods stores used to try to prevent shoplifting.

Candy dances to a music that isn't there. Mandy rocks back and forth on her bunk like an autistic child.

In another letter from the Galveston County Jail, we learned how a group of visitors walked through the inmates' "living room."

At one point in the afternoon there was the announcement for us to 'rack down.' (This term means for everyone to go sit on the bunks.) We were told that, of all things, a 'tour' was coming through and that we should be very still while the tourists were inside the pod. Sure enough, after we were on our bunks, about twenty people filed into the midst of our humble dwelling. I could not figure out what reason they had for coming to the jail. There was a combination of men and women, old and young, and they were dressed up. The ladies carried purses. It looked as if it could just as easily have been a tour of an old historic home as a tour of a jail. As the tourists filed in they looked at us warily. I felt like I was in a zoo.

Marilyn and I were ready for Carolyn to be settled into what we hoped would be a more stable environment, not realizing how many equally difficult challenges she would face in doing prison time. Meanwhile, as I followed the unrelenting struggle of the psalmists against their enemies, John Milton's version of Psalm 6 offered me an assurance of command with which to address the uncertainties we faced as a family over what might happen next.

> Depart from me, for the voice of my weeping
> The Lord hath heard; the Lord hath heard my prayer;
> My supplication with acceptance fair
> The Lord will own, and have me in his keeping.

THE STATE JAIL

Texas houses a large number of offenders in what are called state jails. While these facilities contain primarily fourth-degree felony probationers, they are also temporary locations for housing prisoners carrying more serious offenses who will eventually be moved to what the Texas Department of Criminal Justice (TDCJ) calls "units." The state jails offer no educational opportunities beyond the high school General Equivalency Diploma (GED) conducted by the prison school district and vocational classes for those lacking a high school diploma.

After I received confirmation of Carolyn's arrival at the Lucile G. Plane State Jail near Dayton, Texas, I was not told when we could visit because she had yet to be assigned a TDCJ identification number. When I asked about visitation, I was told that only one visit was allowed per weekend and that approved visitors, consisting of no more than two adults and four children, are allowed two-hour visits. In addition, I was told that we would not be able to receive a contact visit (being seated at a table together) for ninety days.

After her arrival at the L.G. Plane State Jail, a letter from Carolyn described how correctional officers there made a big issue out of whether to allow her to keep her contact lenses. They expressed concern that the lenses might alter the natural color of her eyes. As a result, they made her take out both contact lenses and then put one in, before making the final decision. Four officers looked at her eyes and, after much deliberation, voted that she could keep her contacts.

Carolyn's first job at the L.G. Plane State Jail was sorting clothing in the "sweat shop," a building aptly named because it lacked air conditioning. Her second job was maintenance work that included plumbing and painting chores. She had the good fortune of being exempt from the field work, called "hoe squad" duty, because her medical record specified no long periods of exposure to the sun. A letter to us contained these summary descriptions:

> There is no air conditioning in any of the dorms. When the guards make their rounds they wear wet towels around their necks. We are 'fed' in an assembly line process and are given a maximum of ten minutes to eat. If the chow hall is crowded we are only allowed five minutes.

As we visited with Carolyn one Saturday at the Plane State Jail, she mentioned the task the maintenance crew had of cleaning out the septic tank. One member of the crew was lowered into what was called the "pit" while holding a rope and a bucket. There, in the midst of stifling heat and terrible odor, the work was accomplished. During our visit the following Saturday, Carolyn described her experience of having to "go down" into the pit. She told us that it was all she could do to keep from passing out. The inner pain I felt over what Carolyn was enduring could be compared to what the psalmists felt as they experienced the bitterness of abandonment. I also thought about how we tend to associate "good times" with the presence of God with us and the "bad times" with the absence of God from us. And yet, after the first wave of our grief subsided, a new hope in God was positively awakened. God had heard our anguished cries from the pit of desolation and had raised us up together from its depths. A song of praise accompanied our release from despair.

I waited patiently for the Lord; he inclined to me and heard my cry.
He drew me up from the desolate pit, out of the miry bog,
and set my feet upon a rock, making my steps secure.
He put a new song in my mouth, a song of praise to our God

—Psalm 40:2–3

A DEEPER REFLECTION ON CHAINS

*Untwisting all the chains
that tie the hidden soul of harmony.*[2]

—John Milton

The word "chain" can be used in a deeper sense than that which is conveyed by the physical binding that offenders endure on their travels from one place to another. The chaining of the human spirit is both sad and troublesome. There are those in jail and prison whose spirits are easily defeated and, as a result, are quickly bound by the madness that surrounds them day and night. Their loud voices may be heard in front of a day room TV or during a domino game but, in reality, their chains leave them with no voice of inner strength and no hope for the future. Some make friends with their chains in such a way that freedom from them would be traumatic, like having a security blanket yanked away. The indignity of being chained mirrors the punishment objective of serving time in prison. Such a measure exists, as with so many others, in the name of security. Those who must administer this form of control are limited themselves by various chains of human weakness and so both prisoner and jailer are prospects for receiving the gift of new life. Neither is lost from the searching eyes of the One in whom we live, move, and have our being. To have one's chains "untwisted," one's eyes opened, and God's pardon received, is good news.

FROM GATESVILLE TO MARLIN

Carolyn mailed a letter to us in which we learned that she had been taken to the Gatesville Unit in Central Texas. This facility serves as a reception unit for women who are officially beginning their prison time in Texas. During the approximately six weeks that women spend at this facility they undergo round after round of questioning and tests in order to determine their "classification." The information obtained from them subsequently follows them wherever they are sent within the state. In talking by telephone with a Gatesville Unit employee, I learned that we would not be allowed to visit Carolyn during this phase of her prison time.

2. Milton, "L'Allegro," lines 143–44.

After a few weeks, I called the Gatesville Unit to ask when we might expect Carolyn to be moved to a more permanent location. An employee in the Records Department told me she had already been transferred. She went on to explain that we would be able to visit her the next weekend at the William P. Hobby Unit near Marlin, Texas.

When Carolyn arrived at the Hobby Unit, it was only a short time before her first Christmas in prison. I sent her a copy of the following poem by Gerard Manley Hopkins.

> Moonless darkness stands between.
> Past, the Past, no more be seen!
> But the Bethlehem star may lead me
> To the sight of him who freed me
> From the self that I have been.
> Make me pure, Lord: Thou art holy;
> Make me meek, Lord: Thou wert lowly;
> Now beginning, and alway:
> Now begin, on Christmas day.[3]

3. Hopkins, "Moonless darkness stands between," 170. Used by permission of Oxford University Press on behalf of the British Province of the Society of Jesus.

3

Hurting and Healing

How long must I bear pain in my soul;
and have sorrow in my heart all day long?

—Psalm 13:2a

JERUSALEM WAS DEEPLY WOUNDED, its streets deserted and its temple destroyed. Where laughter and pleasant conversation were once heard, and where songs of Zion were sung so joyously, now there was only the sound of weeping and the slow cadences of weariness and loss. For those left behind, memories would remain of family members and friends who were taken away into captivity, perhaps lost to them forever. The psalmist, hurting and in despair, laments:

But I am like the deaf, I do not hear;
like the mute, who cannot speak.

—Psalm 38:13

Overwhelmed by grief, another psalmist recovers his voice and protests,

How long, O Lord? Will you forget me forever?
How long will you hide your face from me?

—Psalm 13:1

HURTING

Families with a loved one who has just been convicted of committing a serious crime cannot imagine, during the first few days, how they can get through such an ordeal. Some, with feelings of shame and disgrace,

29

lack the confidence to talk to anyone about what they are going through. Many decide to keep it secret or simply do not know anyone with whom they can share the shock and disappointment. This kind of trouble causes fears, uncertainties, and a hurting that is hard to describe. Hopkins' poetic expression of grief gets to the heart of the matter.

> No worst, there is none. Pitched past pitch of grief,
> More pangs will, schooled at forepangs, wilder wring.
> Comforter, where, where is your comforting?
> Mary, mother of us, where is your relief?[1]

The hurting of family members over having a loved one who is heading off to prison often reveals itself through self-condemnation or self-pity. While I continued to struggle with the seriousness of Carolyn's trouble, I thought about the ways I might have failed her. In seeking relief, I found an answer in a little book written by Dietrich Bonhoeffer that eased the burden of such troubling reflections.

> It is thoroughly unbiblical and destructive to think that we can never suffer innocently as long as some error still lies hidden within us.[2]

The effort to cheer someone up who is suffering from the sorrow of a loved one's criminal action is often met by a blank stare. The pain, experienced in different ways by each person affected, is hard for others to understand. Too often, in trying to think of what to say, people end up saying the wrong things. They stammer, offer weak assurances, and fail to offer any sign of God's peace. The most appreciated response comes from the quiet assurance of special friends and their offer of being available in whatever way might be helpful. Marilyn and I were fortunate to be associated with men and women with character who demonstrated in their own lives an abiding trust in the mercies of God. They gave us confidence, not by seeking to offer consolation to us, but simply through their witness of love. Within the body of believers called church, they listened to us.

The twin sentiments of anger and resentment keep many families from considering support possibilities. Friends turn away from them because of their moodiness and their steadfast refusal to be comforted.

---

1. Hopkins, "No worst, there is none. Pitched past pitch of grief," 100. By permission of Oxford University Press on behalf of the British Province of the Society of Jesus.

2. Bonhoeffer, *Psalms*, 54.

Bitterness becomes a daily poison and health is jeopardized. Some who are going through this isolating experience remain silent and sadly out of touch with reality. Others dash wildly from one thing to another like a bird frantically seeking a way to escape from an unexpected enclosure.

Bad habits can be formed out of the strain of having a loved one in jail or prison. Limited contacts with friends, staying away from public gatherings, becoming careless of personal appearance, and forgetting how to smile are just a few of the pitfalls. When anyone asks, "How are you doing?" the reply is often "fine" or "okay," when nothing could be farther from the truth.

Men and women who have loved ones in prison sometimes speak of poor treatment by supervisors and co-workers on their jobs. Their children often have trouble in school and lose friends. Neighbors avoid them and silent glances become as hurtful as words. As the psalmist lamented:

> *My friends and companions stand aloof from my affliction,*
> *and my neighbors stand far off.*
>
> —Psalm 38:11

Family relationships can become strained when a loved one goes to prison. Parents, for example, may not provide enough attention to other children or to each other. Instances of provocation, such as when a parent impatiently calls out to a child, "If you don't straighten up you're going to end up in prison like your brother" occur too often. They can lead a child to become angry, resentful, and withdrawn.

Parents of a son or daughter in prison may attempt to place the blame on each other. Disagreements can lead to distrust and, finally, to serious forms of alienation. Other complications arise when the father or mother of someone in prison remarries and their new partner has no sympathy for the incarcerated son or daughter.

In a marriage where either the husband or the wife goes to prison, problems often develop when the spouse left at home has the sole responsibility of earning a living and caring for the children. Fidelity is an issue, especially when a long sentence is being served. The divorce rate of prison inmates and their spouses is very high. Following a divorce, prisoners are more likely to re-offend when they are released. The next marriage of their former spouse is likely to fail. In addition, children of offenders often end up in prison themselves.

Marilyn, in fulfilling a resolution of faithfulness, identified with mothers who were living through the experience of having a loved one in prison. In the company of women who shared a similar grief experience, they talked openly about how they were affected. They referred to shortness of breath, tightness in the chest and throat, a sick stomach, weakness, and depression. While heaviness of heart and fatigue seem common to this unexpected kind of trouble, nothing marks such sadness as graphically as someone who is trying to speak but whose painfully constricted throat will not permit the passage of sound. Marilyn and I observed how women respond to the experience of having a loved one in prison differently from men. Women are more open than men in their expressions of shock and sadness and are more likely to become involved with support opportunities. They tend to cry more easily and the crying helps them to get through the difficult times. Men, on the other hand, will keep the hurt inside and seek ways to avoid discussing the matter. I became able, in time, to find an opening for conversation with men who appeared resigned to silence and whose faces revealed unmistakable signs of anger.

A hurting that haunts the lives of many of those in prison comes from fathers who were never available to them in a positive way. The failure of fathers to support their families has terribly negative consequences. Men father children in and out of wedlock and abandon the mothers who then have a hard time bringing up the children. Many of those in prison were once victims of childhood abuse at the hands of their fathers. Quite a few were involved in crimes with fathers who used them as accomplices. As one Father's Day approached, I received a special card from Carolyn. Underneath the printed words, she wrote:

> There were not enough Mother's Day cards to go around here at the Hobby Unit. However, that was not the case with Father's Day cards. They are plentiful—an excessive supply. I'm afraid the reason is a sad one. Many of the women here do not have fathers in their lives. Many have never even known their fathers. As I realize that and think about it, I wonder how it can possibly be that I am so fortunate. I deserve nothing, yet I have everything. I love you so very much.

Holidays, such as Thanksgiving and Christmas, are especially hard when a loved one is in prison. In remembering happy times spent together on special days, including birthdays and anniversaries, a shadow is cast over their observance. Thinking about the loved one in prison, and wondering if he or she is remembering good times with the family, can contribute to the sadness of those who supportively wait for their day of release.

The hurting felt by family members of those in prison includes not knowing all of what their loved one is going through day by day. Many who live behind the razor wire do not like to disturb family members with stories of what is happening to them and around them in prison. There are some things, I suspect, that are just too shameful, too foul, or too personally upsetting to relate to loved ones.

Dietrich Bonhoeffer, during his imprisonment by the Nazis during World War II, wrote many letters to his family and friends. His thoughts, as conveyed in these letters, were pleasant and optimistic in order to prevent those close to him from grieving excessively over what he was enduring. But, to his confidant and close ministerial associate, Eberhard Bethge, he occasionally revealed what a hard time he was having. On December 15, 1943, Bonhoeffer wrote:

> At last I should have to start telling you that, in spite of everything that I have written so far, things here are revolting, that my grim experiences often pursue me into the night and that I can shake them off only by reciting one hymn after another, and that I'm apt to wake up with a sigh rather than with a hymn of praise to God.[3]

The "sundown syndrome," as I call it, is hard on many of those in jail or prison. When the sun goes down and the noise level is reduced to murmurs and snores, perhaps a shout or cry, or, at times, a blaring announcement over a loudspeaker, a deeper sadness slips into the minds of all but the most hardened.

The trials of having a loved one in prison are not easily reconciled. Sometimes there is a bitterness that makes speaking difficult and singing impossible. Sometimes God is blamed. Much of the time, supporters wearily pull themselves forward to their next destination. This is what is called "getting by." Then, quite unexpectedly, there comes a brief respite from this prison-conditioned weariness. A message of love arrives from a close friend. A place of peace is found where the road being traveled becomes a little easier to negotiate. Songs of faith, heard during a long night of despair, become harbingers of a new tomorrow. They do not bring the

---

3. Bonhoeffer, *Letters and Papers from Prison*, 162. Reprinted with permission of Scribner, an imprint of Simon & Shuster Adult Publishing Group, copyright© 1953, 1967, 1971 by SCM Press, Ltd.

separation to an end but they can be part of the "rest upon the way"[4] that helps to replenish the strength needed to keep going.

HEALING

Then they cried to the Lord in their trouble
and he saved them from their distress;
he sent out his word and healed them,
and delivered them from destruction.

—Psalm 107:19–20

When a loved one goes to prison, family members who are able to connect to a spirituality common to the psalms have the best chance of finding their way through the grief. We lived through times of feeling "utterly spent and crushed" (Ps 38:8a) and then, after being brought up "from the desolate pit" (Ps 40:2a), "(God) put a new song in (our) mouth(s), a song of praise to our God" (Ps 40:3a). Prayer took on a different meaning for me as the result of being in a marginal position in the world. I realized, in the midst of trouble, that just a prayerful attitude or broadly inclusive prayers would not suffice for the need that was ours. I wanted a special audience with God in order to plead our case. Then, as I gradually felt more at peace, I acknowledged with gratitude the blessing of God's openness to my prayers, much as the psalmist did when he declared, "He has heard the voice of my supplications" (Ps 28:6). Claus Westermann offers us an explanation of this verse.

> This word changes the one speaking. The one who speaks now has been transformed by God's having heard his supplication.[5]

In a later passage, Westermann reveals how lamentation and petition can change into praise in the same psalm as God hears our prayers and answers our calls for help..

> It should be noted that the grief over which the suppliant is lamenting, and for the removal of which he pleads with God, still remains. During the praying of these Psalms no miracle has occurred, but

4. From the hymn, "Beneath the Cross of Jesus," written by Elizabeth C. Clephane.
5. Westermann, *Praise and Lament*, 70.

something else has occurred. God has heard and inclined himself to the one praying. God has had mercy on him.[6]

Thomas Merton once wrote that "Suffering becomes good by accident, by the good it enables us to receive more abundantly from the mercy of God."[7] As we slowly became more experienced travelers on the road that runs through jails and prisons, God's mercy enabled us to be instrumental in helping others through the darkness of their journeys and into the pathway of hope and courage. In the words of the prophet Isaiah:

> *The people who walked in darkness*
> *have seen a great light; those who lived*
> *in a land of deep darkness on them light has shined.*

—Isaiah 9:2

The cross of Jesus, as the revelation of God's love for us, offers us communion with the saints. We are provided a place with those whose similar exposure to a world of grief and shame has helped them to know what God's gift of suffering love can do for them. Henri Nouwen suggested that "Community arises where the sharing of pain takes place, not as a stifling form of self-complaint, but as a recognition of God's saving promises."[8] The Sacrament of Holy Communion (The Lord's Supper) is a part of who we are as God's faithful people. In the light of Jesus' imminent suffering and death, he offered his disciples a specific command: "Do this in remembrance of me" (Luke 22:19, 1 Cor 11:24–25). Our obedience to this request lifts us to a place of spiritual awareness in which what has been lost is found within the saving mercies of the broken body and the shed blood.

Singing is able to ease the strain and stress that comes into the lives of those who care for a loved one in prison. In his sermon, "Songs in Prison," G. Campbell Morgan, a renowned preacher from the early years of the last century, proclaimed:

> Christianity does not say what cannot be cured must be endured, it says rather, *these things must be endured because they are part of the cure.* These things are to be cheerfully borne because they have the strange and mystic power to make whole and strong, and so lead

6. Ibid., 79.

7. Merton, *No Man Is An Island*, 78.

8. Nouwen, *The Wounded Healer*, 94.

35

to victory and the final glory. Christianity as an experience is the ability to know that this will be so, even while the agony is upon us, and so we are able to sing in the midst of it.[9]

The regular worship of God, including the private devotion of prayer, offers healing to hurting hearts. When other words seem weak and empty, The Lord's Prayer opens a way to the presence of God. The Jesus prayer, repeated over and over, "Lord Jesus Christ, have mercy on me," can be of help during times of worry and restlessness when we need to be still.

I officially retired from my years of ministry in 1997. By that time, Marilyn and I were active members of the Texas Inmate Families Association (TIFA). In addition, we aligned ourselves with those engaged in prison ministry under the faith umbrella of the Restorative Justice Ministry Network as well as the Criminal Justice and Mercy Ministries Committee of the Texas Annual Conference of the United Methodist Church. The association we established with these groups kept us from experiencing the kind of pain that isolates and immobilizes many of those who try to "go it alone" through the experience of having a loved one in prison. We were repeatedly blessed by how faithfully they held us up in prayer and helped us to learn about the various ministries to prisoners and those who care for them.

In response to the increased time we gained through my retirement, Marilyn and I began to seek ways through which hope and healing were being experienced by those affected by a loved one's prison time. One such program allowed wives inside the prison to be with their husbands for a guided weekend experience. We heard personal accounts of reconciliation and renewal that came from allowing husbands and wives to visit with each other, to eat together, pray together, and cry together.

We learned about programs that help to limit the risk children of offenders have of becoming criminals. One of the most important, sponsored by prison ministry groups and churches, is summer camps for children of men and women in prison. In addition, there are children whose experience of having a parent in prison is eased by a program in Texas called the Storybook Project. Volunteers record the voices of offenders reading stories and then mail these recordings and companion books to their children. Children of women offenders in the prisons around

---

9. Morgan, "Songs in Prison," 62–63. Compiled and Edited by Richard Morgan, Howard Morgan, and John Morgan and used with their permission.

Gatesville, Texas, were the first to benefit from this program. Later, it was expanded through TIFA to include a men's prison near Huntsville.

No More Victims is a unique school connection with youth who have a mother or father in prison. Marilyn Gambrell, a former parole officer, obtained permission from the principal of Smiley High School in Smiley, Texas, to start a special class for these troubled students. The results have been amazing. In a school district with many problem students, the spirit with which these particular students commit to each other and to a better way of life for themselves has brought the program national attention.

A program called Kairos Outside provides women in and around Houston who have a loved one in prison the opportunity to get together once a year. The attendees have every possible courtesy extended to them and are able, for a little while, to let the tears of hurting flow in the presence of unconditional love. Marilyn attended this special Kairos event at a pleasant location just west of Houston. She sympathized with those who experienced great hardship and appreciated the volunteers who offered love and acceptance to those whose needs are often unknown.

Our visits with Carolyn every other weekend were adventures of faith. With Van visiting on the other weekends, she received a visit every week. At the beginning, however, our visits held notes of sadness and uncertainty. We would drive away from the Hobby Unit saying very little, sometimes close to tears, but always sensing in a special way what the other was thinking. Our spirits took wing as the fog from Carolyn's former dependencies lifted and was replaced by a clearer perspective of who she was and to whom she belonged.

Not long after Carolyn arrived at the Hobby Unit, Gary Whitbeck, the United Methodist minister who became her mentor and friend, began his monthly visits. All of us were grateful for his dedication in driving long distances to visit with Carolyn and, in the process, to help her gain the confidence she needed in order to move beyond the crippling aspects of her guilt.

Marilyn and I reached a point where we began to take advantage of the occasional opportunities to have Polaroid pictures taken with Carolyn during visitation time. This prison-sponsored program allowed a visitation officer to take the pictures and collect three dollars for each one. At the beginning of the prison years, we were somewhat turned-off by the idea of having pictures taken with our daughter dressed in white prison clothes. Then, after a few years, the picture taking assumed a special importance. During holiday seasons, there were decorations on the wall that served as a background to pictures taken with loved ones and friends. They were able to show a softer side of prison.

The three of us, while caring for Carolyn, also took time to care for each other. We regularly provided for each other a steady and reliable source of conversational pleasure and relief. We lingered on subjects that spoke of a bountiful world, a world of goodness and truth, a world of light-hearted banter, of games, of gardens, and gatherings, of food, of the master artist's cloud formations, and musical side trips down memory lane. Reports about our daily activities, including the work we had begun with family members who had loved ones in jail or prison, were shared at the visitation table with Carolyn and through our letters to her. Our conversations did not require advance planning. They arose out of heartfelt assurance that, through God's attention to us, we were "victors in the midst of strife."[10]

Carolyn reached a point in her prison time where she was accepted, and her special ways affirmed, by correctional officers. In both her work skills and her attitude, they recognized her as someone special. One day, three correctional officers provided unusual assistance in getting her to the clinic for emergency medical attention. After I learned of that incident, I wrote to the warden to tell her what they had done and to ask if she would convey our appreciation to them. At our next visit, we learned how thrilled they were to receive a commendation from the warden. As I thought back on the winter trips we made to visit Carolyn, I wrote:

> Winter is a hard time of the year to visit a loved one in prison. There are ominous skies, sometimes turning loose bone-chilling rain. Sometimes there are bright skies and bitter cold. Uncomfortable travel weather can push feelings into a deeper sadness zone. In addition, lifelessness is reflected in the dull colors of the winter landscape along the roads many of us travel to prisons.
>
> Winter reminds me of the coldness of prison life in ways that touch everyone involved. Waiting on the outside for our visit, I think of our daughter, exposed to the penetrating cold of a Texas 'norther.' Linked to every kind of fear and worry family members have over an incarcerated loved one, I think about the possibility that she could get sick without having the kind of medical attention those of us on the outside take for granted. It is only after we enter the visitation area, and the allotted two hours speeds by, that my winter fears subside.

10. From the hymn, "Joyful, Joyful, We Adore Thee," written by Henry Van Dyke.

Each visit we make to the William P. Hobby Unit includes an informal ritual of affirmation and acceptance, an unrehearsed celebration of family solidarity.

We have a prayer and name the blessings of life, reflecting honestly on how we are doing, inside and outside. Our conversation is interspersed with laughter and prayerful expressions and, sometimes, tears. At the beginning and at the close of our contact visits (sitting at a table together), Marilyn and I offer a warm embrace to this 'child of our household' as the fire of unbounded love burns away the lingering chill of winter and the hurting subsides.

We will return, no matter how many more seasons along this familiar highway we must travel, buoyed by a confident answer to the poet's question, 'If winter comes, can spring be far behind?'[11]

Martin Marty's reflections on the winter of the heart warned me against being too confident about springtime relief. He writes:

The wind of furious winter for a while blows without, and then grows silent as spring comes. The fury and the bleakness within the soul can remain, no matter what the season or the weather.[12]

Family members, whose loyalty does not depend on special seasons and who put no limits upon the inconveniences of travel, drive the roads and highways across the nation to visit loved ones in prison. The heaviness of this responsibility intensifies as loved ones age and health problems make visits increasingly difficult. On behalf of all who make long trips to prison to visit loved ones, these words from a familiar Christmas hymn speak beautifully of Christian hope.

And ye, beneath life's crushing load,
whose forms are bending low,
Who toil along the climbing way with painful steps and slow,
Look now! for glad and golden hours come swiftly on the wing.
O rest beside the weary road, and hear the angels sing!
—Edmund H. Sears

11. From the poem, "Ode to a Skylark," written by Percy Bysshe Shelley.
12. Marty, *Cry of Absence*, 2.

4

Prison

*We find in prison those who have gone to negative extremes in society
seeking to be understood in a place that has little capacity or empathy to
respond. Prisons unquestionably need order, and yet, by their very nature
they threaten all order. In essence, they are societies of pain,
confusion and anger.[1]*

—Henry Covert

PRISONS EXIST TO SEGREGATE and control the lives of those who commit crimes. Much of what prison is supposed to correct relates to
what has gone wrong in human relations, in business, and in communities. People from all walks of life do things that make the punishment of
prison both necessary and tragic.

The understanding that prison inflicts serious damage upon human
lives has been revealed in a variety of studies. Two books about prison
that can stimulate discussion of the subject are *The Lucifer Effect* and
American Furies.[2]

Philip Zimbardo's book, *The Lucifer Effect: Understanding How Good
People Become Evil,* graphically illustrates the results of the Stanford
Prison Experiment of 1971 involving students who were paid $15.00 a
day to participate. The conclusion reached was that good people, in pos-
ing as prison guards in a mock prison setting, could become horribly as-
sertive and ingenious in their abuse of those who were acting the part of
prisoners in the experiment. Although the results of the Stanford Prison

1. Covert, *Ministry to the Incarcerated,* 17.

2. *The Lucifer Effect* and *American Furies* as reviewed by Michael Berryhill, School of
Communication, University of Houston, appeared in the "Zest" section of the Houston
Chronicle on Sunday, August 12, 2007.

Experiment were published, Zimbardo could not bring himself to write a book about it until photographs taken inside Iraq's Abu Ghraib Prison in 2004, depicting abuse and torture, were made available to the world.

Sasha Abramsky's book, *American Furies: Crime, Punishment and Vengeance in the Age of Mass Imprisonment,* goes into detail about the various costs of warehousing prisoners. It presents, along with a history of prisons, facts pertaining to how prisons drain off exorbitant sums of state money, sacrificing public health and education, much of it on behalf of undeserved forms of punishment.

Prisons cannot be expected to send large numbers of offenders back into the world as better people. Joseph Hallinan illustrates the point that rehabilitation is, for the most part, unsuccessful.

> A former Texas inmate named Race Sample told me you couldn't rehabilitate a man if he had never been habilitated in the first place. And many inmates never have been. They've never had those basic things that most of us would probably agree are essential to developing a decent human being: a loving home, a decent education, a faith of some kind. To expect a man to find these things in prison is, on most days, laughable. Prison is the wrong place to try to habilitate anybody. The level of violence and fear and degradation that permeates most prisons makes a luxury of everything but survival. But not trying is even worse. The absence of effort creates a vacuum, and the vacuum is filled by baser considerations. Profit is one. Indifference is another.[3]

The argument that everything about prison decreases dignity and increases despair is compelling. However, there are stories about overcoming prison that are not told often enough. Hope enters the lives of some prisoners through the work and witness of God's agents of rescue and renewal who sing the good news of freedom in Christ.

U. S. PRISONS

The prison population of eighteenth-century England received brutal treatment. Prisoners were regularly executed by hanging for their crimes. In order to ease the problem of overcrowded prisons, the British Parliament passed the Transportation Act in 1718 that resulted in noncapital offenders being transported to the colonies of America.

3. Hallinan, *Going Up the River,* 216.

East Granby, Connecticut, is generally accepted as the location of the first prison in America. Named after London's famous Newgate Prison, it first served as a political prison during the Revolutionary War.[4] The Walnut Street Jail was built in Philadelphia around 1790 as an experiment designed to turn prisoners into penitents. The Quaker theory from which it derived connected solitary reading of the scriptures to the kind of religious instruction that would move prisoners to repent of their sins. The guards did not carry weapons and corporal punishment was forbidden. The loneliness and misery of the Walnut Street Jail isolation technique drove many of the prisoners mad.

The prison at Auburn, New York, located in the Finger Lakes region of the state, was built in 1797. The so-called Auburn system became the architectural model (tiers set within a large open frame) for much prison building that followed. The prisoners at Auburn worked during the day and kept a strict regimen of silence. The management purpose was to break each prisoner's spirit as a prelude to meaningful reform.

Sing Sing Prison, opened in 1828, derived its unusual name from its location at Ossining, New York. A punishment practice of its first years of operation was absolute silence with beatings administered for those who failed to comply. The phrase, "being sent up the river" originated from the large number of convicted criminals being sent from New York City up the Hudson River to Sing Sing.

Another well-known Quaker experiment, first called Cherry Hill, opened in Philadelphia in 1829. Later named Eastern State Penitentiary, it was an architectural marvel that attracted up to 10,000 visitors a year. Prisoners were never allowed to leave their cells. The expected result was that physical isolation would cause them to "lose all their guilty stains."[5] However, this static regimen was not successful. Complaints regularly surfaced over the cruelty associated with such limited human contact. Eastern State closed in 1971 and is now a National Historic Landmark.

The California State Prison at San Quentin, north of San Francisco, was built in 1852 to house 3,317 inmates. In 1930, it was listed as the largest prison in the world with more than 6,000 inmates. Through the years, San Quentin's ways of dealing with prisoners has encompassed a

4. I have several postcards of Old Newgate Prison showing the year of its origin as 1773. Carolyn gave me these cards after her release from prison.

5. From the hymn, "There Is a Fountain Filled with Blood," written by William Cowper.

wide range of therapeutic models. Finally, placing television sets in the cells brought greater peace to the prison population without incurring an exorbitant program expense.

Elmira, New York, was the location of a prison camp for Confederate soldiers during the Civil War. Afterward, in 1876, it became the first "reformatory" in America. Elmira Reformatory introduced the "indeterminate sentence" in which the prisoners were subjected to several different treatment regimes. A system of rewards and punishments was expected to motivate them into making right choices. After a period of good behavior, the prisoner was released on parole. The reformatory system went so far as to call inmates "patients." Several prisons in America copied the Elmira model in an attempt to reform prisoners, but the experiment was not successful.

After the Civil War, prison time became nothing more than a terribly punishing holding action. With the depletion of maintenance funds, all social control experiments in prison ended and they became little more than horrible places of punishment. At the same time, the leasing of convicts expanded and the use of chain gangs became a common practice. Former slaves, enduring harsher and more restrictive conditions as convicts, sang songs of the plantation to help them endure the pain.

The Kentucky State Penitentiary, widely known as the "Castle on the Cumberland," was completed in 1889 at a cost of $275,000. Located within a short distance of the Cumberland River, the prison was built by stonemasons from Italy. It currently houses Kentucky's most violent offenders. Inside, the old fortress-like structure employs the use of state of the art security equipment. Outside, above the entrance door, there is a sign that reads, "Abandon Hope, All Ye That Enter Here."

A few of the country's older prisons occupy special places in prison lore because of how they were designed. Some of their names call to mind the terror and violence that took place within their walls, while others are notable because of how they were managed. The federal prison in Leavenworth, Kansas, opened in 1906 after being built by its first inmate occupants. Sue Titus Reid describes how it happened in the fourth edition of her book on criminal justice.

> The first federal prison was taken over from the War Department at Fort Leavenworth, Kansas. The facility had been used to house military offenders. It was found to be inadequate for the federal system and Congress authorized the building of a prison on the

Fort Leavenworth military reservation. Federal offenders housed at Fort Leavenworth built the prison. On 1 February 1906, inmates were moved to the new prison and Fort Leavenworth was returned to the War Department.[6]

The well-known federal prison Alcatraz opened in 1934. Located on an island called "the Rock," its purpose was to incarcerate the most dangerous federal offenders. It was there that a man named Robert F. Stroud, because of his knowledge of bird diseases, became known as the "Birdman of Alcatraz." There are no confirmed records of successful escape attempts from Alcatraz. Closed in 1963, it has become the most frequently visited tourist attraction in the San Francisco area.

Prisons of somewhat later design that possess special characteristics and stand out in prison history include Statesville, Illinois, with its circular cell houses; Attica, New York, with a death toll of 43 in its 1971 riot; and Angola, Louisiana, with its long-tenured Warden Burl Cain. How they are visually perceived is much different from the "modern correctional facility" described by Joseph T. Hallinan as "a concrete econo-box, low and bunkered and anonymous."[7]

Riots and escape attempts mark the pages of prison history in the United States. The outbreaks of prison violence in the late sixties and early seventies are thought to have been the result of prisoners imagining their strife and tension to be connected to the problems the country itself was going through. The prisoners picked up on how war and racism were inflaming partisan sentiment outside of the prisons.

Prisons in the United States at the turn of the century were showing signs of drastic overcrowding. Statistics regularly appearing in newspaper reports revealed that the number of incarcerated men and women in the United States was greater than countries with larger population totals. In spite of the sad truth of how poorly we have done as a nation in keeping people out of prison, we should not forget how prison can be credited for providing important wake-up calls to some of those whose mistakes took them to unexpected levels of trouble. Prison is, therefore, even in its institutional madness, a place from which the lost ones may, through ways only God can know, find the right direction home. Indeed, where love and sorrow meet within such places of confinement, there are those

6. Reid, *Criminal Justice*, 4th edition, 339.
7. Hallinan, *Going Up the River*, xvii.

who respond to the call of freedom in the spirit represented in "Depth of Mercy," Charles Wesley's hymn of confession and repentance.

> *There for me the Savior stands, holding forth his bleeding hands;*
> *God is love! I know, I feel, Jesus weeps and loves me still.*

—fourth stanza

PRISON MANAGEMENT

Management problems in jails and prisons
increase the problems of living behind the walls.

—Sue Titus Reid

There is something about prisons that makes effective operation difficult to implement. The perpetual threat of trouble sets people on edge and the uselessness felt by so many of those who live in prison carries over in ways that have a negative effect on everyone. The lack of sufficient accountability is a regular management problem. Jack Cowley, a former prison warden who once directed the work of Prison Fellowship's InnerChange Freedom Initiative at a prison near Houston, was a witness for the Commission on Safety and Abuse in American Prisons. He said, "When we're not held accountable, the culture inside the prisons becomes a place that is so foreign to the culture of the real world that we develop our own way of doing things."[8]

State agencies governing prisons are slow to address the problem of accountability in prisons. I believe this omission relates to how those in authority are inclined to let prison do what prison does through whatever ways, within budget limits, each warden chooses. Because the prison reflects many of the same cultural aberrations of the "real world," I wonder how much of what is called "our own way of doing things" is just another accommodation to the easiest way to get employees to do a job not many people will accept. Or, could it be a way to keep those for whom any change from the old way of doing things would mean trouble? An uncommon

8. Gibbons and Katzenbach, "Confronting Confinement," 81. Gibbons and Katzenbach co-chair the Commission on Safety and Abuse in America's Prisons.

leadership plan is needed in order to run prisons in the best way possible. It is far too easy to settle for expediency in a setting where goodness and mercy are not well represented. Carolyn offered us her observations about a typical prison inspection.

> The system attempts to portray a semblance of order. It is almost humorous to observe the events taking place when one of the state executives is scheduled to visit or when an audit is about to take place. From the position of the executive on the prison unit, the beauty is that no one visits by surprise. All visits by outsiders are arranged in advance and adjustments can be made to ensure that a no nonsense image is in place. Ranking officials, even wardens, make rounds ever so often, but again, even at the unit level, the system of notification is extremely reliable and hardly ever allows for a surprise visit. When the warden or ranking official sets foot into the interior of the compound, telephones start ringing in a domino effect reaction. The officer at the post where the official crosses into the interior of the compound starts the chain of notification and each notified post notifies the next. Therefore, the result is a semblance of order. When the official arrives at each building, officers are at their assigned posts on diligent patrol. Inmates react, as well. Clothes are pulled off of the walls where they are hanging, loitering in the aisles ceases and everyone scatters in order to present a picture of compliance. No one ever gets to see how it really is. There is one way, and only one way, to really know what goes on, day by day, year after year, inside a prison and no one in t h e i r right mind is going to pay the price of admission for the purpose of finding out.

The question is often asked, "Who would want to work in a prison?" The questioners may not realize that many of those in positions of management have worked their way up from the lowest level of prison employment. Members of the same family are often found doing prison work. They know a lot about prisons and tend to get along well with "convicts." Retired military personnel find that prison work enables them to make use of their former experience. While we have met a few prison employees who think of their work as a public service, the largest number consists of those who simply need a job.

A common assessment of prison management is that the reputation of a prison depends upon the warden. The warden of each prison is known to have practically unlimited authority. There are "hands-on" wardens who are very involved in all that goes on in the prison and there are "administrators" who delegate authority to those who report to them. The warden's influence over a prison, including prisoners, personnel, and programs, has resulted in certain facilities presenting an uncommon face to the world. Such was the case of Sing Sing under the leadership of Warden Lewis Lawes in the first half of the nineteenth century and, years later, Warden Dennis Luther, who provided extraordinary direction to McKean, a federal prison in Bradford, Pennsylvania. Luther, now retired, believed in unconditional respect for inmates as people. Prison criminologist John DiIulio said, "McKean is probably the best managed prison in the country, and that has everything to do with a warden named Dennis Luther."[9]

Luther had twenty-eight "Beliefs About the Treatment of Inmates" that he came up with as the result of his many years as a warden. Here are six of his beliefs:[10]

1. Inmates are sent to prison *as* punishment and not *for* punishment.
2. Correctional workers have a *responsibility* to ensure that inmates are returned to the community no more angry or hostile than when they were committed.
3. Inmates are entitled to a safe and humane environment while in prison.
4. You must believe in a man's *capacity* to change his behavior.
5. Normalize the environment to the extent possible by providing programs, amenities, and services. The denial of such must be related to maintaining order and security rather than punishment.
6. Most inmates will respond favorably to a clean and aesthetically pleasing physical environment and will not vandalize or destroy it.

Inmates at McKean had recreation, work, long-term goals, and incentives, while operational expenses were consistently lower than prisons of comparable size and population. The key, it seems, was attitude and superior management. We can only pray for a miracle sufficient to move the people in charge of our nation's prisons toward "a clearly defined organizational principle, one that articulates the justification and meaning

---

9. Worth, "A Model Prison," lines 60–63.
10. Ibid., lines 102–17.

of punishment, and to which each element of the penal environment is held accountable . . . "[11]

PRISON LIFE

Some sat in darkness and in gloom,
prisoners in misery and in irons,

—Psalm 107:10

Prison life is not soft by any stretch of the imagination. Soft bedding is unheard of, the soft touch of a loved one's hand is often only a memory, and soft answers are seldom ever heard. In addition, there are no soft songs about prison life. In fact, the music of prison regularly presents hard notes for hard times.

Men and women are stripped of their "free world" choices when they go to prison. They do not choose where they will live, what they will wear, who their cellmate will be, or what number will be used to identify them. They do not get to decide what job they will have or what they will be served in the chow hall. They do not have the freedom to determine where they will go or how they will get there. They are ordered about, sometimes cursed and belittled, and quickly learn to call anyone in authority, "boss." They understand that they will be counted, over and over, and that they will be subjected to noise, both day and night. When they first arrive in prison, they may be surprised to learn how many who are already there have stopped thinking about going home.

Sue Titus Reid describes, in her exhaustive text *Criminal Justice*, a subculture that offenders encounter when they come into prison. She credits a man by the name of Donald Clemmer in a study he conducted in 1940, for defining that subculture as "prisonization." The most important aspects of prisonization, she quotes Clemmer as describing, are "the influences which breed or deepen criminality and antisociality and make the inmate characteristic of the ideology in the prison community." She writes:

> The degree to which prisonization is effective in a given inmate depends on several factors: (1) the inmate's susceptibility and personality; (2) the inmate's relationships outside the prison; (3) the

---

11. Skotnicki, *Religion and the Development of the American Penal System*, 141–42.

inmate's membership in a primary group in prison; (4) the inmate's placement in the prison, such as which cell and cellmate; and (5) the degree to which the inmate accepts the dogmas and codes of the prison culture.[12]

Every prison holds offenders who remain conditioned by "free world" versions of the violence they helped to promote before being sent to prison. These individuals use a prisonized version of the threats and demands they employed outside of prison to establish their turf and gain control over others. On the other hand, there are a few who remain brittle and voiceless as the result of some sad derailment of life. They live in the emptiness of unfulfilled desire while "listening to the prisoned cricket shake its terrible, dissembling music in the granite hill."[13]

Tattoos are important to prisoners because of what they reveal to others around them. Some enter prison already marked by body art. Others, after joining the ranks of the incarcerated, engage the services of an inmate tattoo artist. Their personally chosen images—many select a gang symbol—are painfully worked into the skin with makeshift instruments. This kind of business, conducted under various covers, is subject to disciplinary action by the prison.

The clothes men and women are required to put on when they go to prison changes how they feel about themselves as well as how others feel about them. Prison clothes carry a mark of shame that is hard to remove even when, after years of wear, they are taken off. In their various colors from county to county and from state to state, the clothes prisoners wear signify to everyone who comes near them that they are living without the freedom everyone else takes for granted.

The passage of time robs prisoners of a sensory awareness of once familiar tastes and odors. Also, as a visitor, I have noticed how prisoners often become angry, agitated, or greatly disappointed over what they view as bad news, no matter how insignificant it might actually be, while the slightest hint of good news is received with loud exclamations of happiness.

Prison is often described as "a school for crime." Novices are able to take advanced courses in "criminology" from experienced convicts. Carolyn offers the following explanation:

12. Reid, *Criminal Justice*, 7th ed., 284–85.

13. Bogan, "Men Loved Wholly Beyond Wisdom," lines 11–13. Copyright © 1968 Louise Bogan. Copyright renewed by Ruth Limmer. Reprinted by permission of Farrar, Straus, and Giroux, LLC.

By simply listening and observing I now have the knowledge required to set up and run a dope lab. I have overheard detailed discussions about flasks, chemicals, supplies, processes, measurements, and prices, and I did not have any of this information before I came to prison.

Smart "cons" regularly come up with ideas on how to fool the "police," (referring to correctional officers) and that will enable them to obtain contraband (items illegal for them to possess). A few offenders in each prison are self-described "high rollers," throwing security to the wind in obtaining items from the outside through illicit contacts. Others simply dream of being accepted by someone who will give them a little time and attention.

The sounds of prison are permanently recorded in the minds of those who have been around prisons for any length of time. The days and nights are filled with the sounds of buzzing locks and closing gates, of orders being shouted and objections being raised, along with announcements coming out over speaker systems. Offenders and those who watch over them, spinning together in an orbit of conflict and confusion, occasionally are heard speaking to each other in civil tones.

Some of those who live at the far end of the prison population and who have lost all thought of restraint take out their anger on correctional personnel in the worst kinds of ways. At the same time, there are men and women who work for the prison who misuse their authority. Sadly, the requirement of choosing the greater good or, perhaps more often, the lesser evil, is clearly more difficult in a setting where strength of character is lacking and where anger and violence brings fear to those whose lives are on the line.

In one of the letters we received from Carolyn, she offered the following thoughts:

The primary focus of the majority of offenders is 'doing their time' so they can get out. I think it is rare when they even think about what they did to get here in the first place, except for revealing methods. When that is done, it is more along the lines of remembering an 'occupation,' instead of analyzing a downfall in an effort to avoid future failures. Accountability is missing. Remorse is missing. Not in every case, but in so many. An offender can spend years in prison without being confronted even once about their crime. Talking, boasting, comparing—that's one thing—but being confronted is another. That is the missing ingredient in prison. This confrontation sometimes occurs in small doses in a few of the rehab programs and groups but they are often not mandatory and, when they are, it is usually toward the end of one's prison time—prison time that has established within the offender its own distorted belief system.

When the sun sets on each day of life in prison, tears are shed, tears of sadness and regret over lost time and the thought of loved ones whose lives they can only share from a distance. In the face of each prisoner's deepest sorrow, God knows and cares. Within the incomparable suffering of a savior's dying love, there is hope for the prisoner's tomorrow. This kind of hope is embedded in the loneliness of each "dark night of the soul."

MAIL

A prisoner's morale is boosted when mail is received from family and friends. One of the saddest sights in jail or prison is that of inmates who wait eagerly for mail call and who walk away, day after day, without a letter. The feeling they have of being forgotten makes it harder for men and women in prison to imagine a broader, deeper reality. Their narrow world closes in upon them while their longing for familiar contacts continues, sometimes for years. It is hard for them to understand why their family members can't find time to write or, sadly, lack what it takes to put words down on paper.

When I served a time as a volunteer chaplain at the L. G. Plane State Jail for women, I learned that the greatest worry of the women prisoners was not hearing from members of their family. They were deeply concerned about how their children were doing and when they would be able to see them. Some of the letters they received were not satisfying and they would ask for my interpretation of what was written to them. I suggested to these offenders that it was hard for their family members to keep up with all their obligations. I asked them to consider how many commitments their loved ones had, such as caring for *their* children, working late hours, and trying to make ends meet. I wanted them to understand that not getting a letter every few days didn't mean they were not loved. On the other hand, in speaking to family members, I always pointed out the importance of keeping up a regular schedule of writing. The commitment of writing to prisoners by the ones who have the greatest stake in their future is a gift of great magnitude.

Those who are serving time in prison are blessed when they receive letters that hold the promise of prayer and offer encouragement in how they may relate, in faith, to their places of confinement. In addition, mailing stories clipped out of magazines, cross word puzzles, and cartoons keeps prisoners in touch with the outside world and provides ways to help them pass the time. It should be kept in mind that many prisons specify that they can accept only photocopied articles. I heard someone suggest that family members keep several addressed postcards with them and when something noteworthy is seen or heard, no matter where it occurs, a card can be used to jot down a description of the event. Picture postcards from different locations are special. Jorge Antonio Renaud recommends imaginative mailings.

> And by imaginative, I'll tell you what my wife does. She'll buy computer spreadsheets, those long rolls of perforated paper. She'll paint on them colored eggs on Easter, or multicolored balls and trees for Christmas. She'll fold them and send them in a large manila envelope. When they arrive, I unwrap them and wind them all around my cell. Their color and festive design make me know, without a doubt, that someone cared enough to brighten my day, my drab cell—at least until some guard takes them down—with some time and attention.[14]

Family members and friends send news about everyday happenings in their lives. They also send letters of encouragement and the importance of keeping the faith. Unfortunately, prisoners occasionally receive threatening, demanding, and otherwise greatly troubling letters. Letters of personal rejection are received that convey what is called being "kicked to the curb." Many of these notices are hard to bear and add misery to lives already devalued. While I was answering requests from women inmates who had asked to see the chaplain, an offender entered the office holding a letter she asked me, as the volunteer chaplain that day, to read. The letter was from a friend offering sympathy to her on the death of her father. Her family had not thought enough of her to let her know what had happened.

Some prisoners write letters in an attempt to find someone who will write to them. They find addresses of churches and prison ministry groups in the hope of locating a pen pal. Pen-pal relationships between

14. Renaud, *Behind the Walls*, 69.

prisoners and outside contacts have mixed results. Some are positive. Some never reach a desirable level of fulfillment. Carolyn offers the following assessment:

> Many women pass their time through pen-pal relationships with men in the outside world. Often the women write several men at the same time and spend countless hours writing letters designed to obtain a deposit of funds into their commissary account.

Men seek women pen pals for much the same purpose. Some men, as well as women, will start visiting a pen pal in prison. Occasionally, a proxy marriage is the result of what started out as a pen-pal relationship. On the other hand, countless numbers of men and women are played for a fool and deserted.

All mail sent to prisoners, and mail written by prisoners, is closely inspected. Pornographic material, as well as references to crime, drugs, and racial hatred, will not be accepted. Unfortunately, there are those, inside and out, who regularly test the system.

Inmate to inmate correspondence is generally prohibited in state prisons. This prohibition fuels a variety of creative ideas that fulfill the objective of making contact with friends. Some offenders use family members or associates outside of prison to send news or information to those who are serving prison time at another location.

PRISON NAMES AND PRISON LANGUAGE

"Prisoner" is the most common word used by "free world" citizens when they speak of those serving time in prison. Other words include "convict," "inmate," and "offender." Men and women entering prison for the first time are basically indifferent to what they are called. On the other hand, those who have been there for a long time will say, unequivocally, "I am a convict." Carolyn offers the following explanation:

> An 'inmate' or an 'offender' is one who 'just rolled up' and is 'green to the game.' A 'convict' is 'old school,' which demands respect on the inside. A 'convict' minds her own business. Frequently when verbal altercations erupt, name calling involves the terms 'inmate' or 'offender.' A 'snitch' is a prisoner who informs the 'law' against someone else to either get out of trouble or to gain favor. A 'snitch' gets no respect. It is safest and most desirable to be known as a

'convict' inside the walls of a Texas prison. That may sound strange but that's just the way it is in a strange land.

Prison speech tends to establish prison citizenship. There are words, rooted in the prison experience, that are common to the world of the incarcerated everywhere. Profanity is employed shamelessly and certain inoffensive words, possessing a common meaning, have an uncommon meaning in prison. There is even a prison humor that, in its own words, helps to create a defense against depression. Men and women who have been out of prison for awhile are pleased to meet someone outside who speaks the language of prison. This is not much different than returning home from years of living in a foreign country and finding pleasure in meeting a citizen of that country with whom conversation can be shared.

Beyond the common speech of the prison, there exists a spiritually tuned speech of freedom that blows where it will inside the confining enclosures. This expectant language does not come from the managers of the prison, nor is it dependent upon officially sanctioned religious practices. Instead, it springs up from the ancestral wells of awakened souls and is given a voice of hope to share "wonderful words of life," words that "offer pardon and peace to all."[15]

GANGS IN PRISON

The prevalence of gangs and gang activity in prisons is one of the most serious problems with which prison officials have to deal. Gang membership carries a form of social control that is far-reaching and dangerous. For this reason, efforts are made to identify and systematically isolate gang members from each other by placing them in single person cells. Hispanic gangs, often characterized as the most violent and separatist in tendencies, constitute substantially over half of all gang members in prison. The most well organized gangs have bylaws that require the death penalty for members who violate the rules of the gang. "Ratting" is one of the most serious infractions a member can commit against the gang since it involves revealing information about other gang members to the authorities. Prison gang leaders generally choose to remain quiet and stay out of trouble. This serves to keep them in a better position to issue orders related to drug deals and gang membership.

15. From the hymn, "Wonderful Words of Life," written by Philip P. Bliss.

There are men who enter prison as certified members of a gang. Others become candidates for gang affiliation after coming to prison. Different factors such as youth, racial pride, and prison conditions combine to create a combustible mix of anger, abuse, and resentment that opens the door to gang invitations. Sometimes these factors result in individual prisoners being labeled as gang members even when they have not been formally inducted into a gang. For instance, when a number of offenders in a prison assemble together to protest conditions in the prison, there is a chance they may be labeled as gang members.

The racial divide in prison creates, in many locations, serious problems. While gang warfare in prison is often sparked by racial conflict, there are those who contend that the prison system is largely at fault because of the regular use of forced integration. This idea is consistent with the compulsion most prisoners have to protect their turf from anyone who presents a threat to their settled routine, as well as to fiercely resist anything that suggests personal disrespect. Prison authorities are quick to explain that wide-ranging steps are being taken to limit gang proliferation. They tell about programs that encourage and facilitate gang renunciation as well as the policy of private cell confinement (segregation) of gang members.

PRISON VIOLENCE

Violence exists in a prison much like the presence of boiling lava inside a very active volcano. The potential for devastation stirs just beneath the surface at all times. It can erupt over the slightest provocation—or without any recognizable provocation. The physical "fighting" common to prison life often causes injuries and, at times, results in severe disciplinary measures being handed out to the combatants. Anger, prejudice, hopelessness, and a history of violent living touch a large segment of those in prison. Overcrowding, loss of privileges, use of unnecessary force by authorities and, quite often, uncomfortable physical conditions throughout the system, intensifies tempers already frayed to the breaking point. Fists fly over the control rights to contraband sources and threats are made against some of those who refuse to give up a share of their commissary bag.

Carolyn offers the following observation on what takes place in a prison for women:

> In prison, our definition of 'business as usual' includes a mixture of physical fighting, sexual activity, and profane shouting matches.

> The main components of abuse consist of verbal, psychologi-
> cal, and physical violence. Riots are not a significant aspect of a
> prison for women. The one time that a 'riot' was discussed in my
> dorm—the self-appointed leader went from cell to cell in an at-
> tempt to organize the revolt. There were 150 women in that dorm
> and practically the same number of opinions regarding strategy.
> Needless to say, not much happened.

Riots in prisons for men provide opportunities for inmates to settle old scores and protest new threats to their territory. While they are inevitably doomed to fail, they can wreak havoc upon the prison for short periods of time. The retribution these prisoners suffer from achieving no more than a briefly euphoric sense of "sticking it to the man" (anyone who assumes authority) is costly.

Rape is one of the most serious acts of violence in prisons for men and one of the hardest to control. While homosexuality is often cited by prison officials and prison ministry volunteers as the root cause of rape in prison, there is no valid evidence to support that suggestion. A book whose authors possess extensive inside knowledge of prisons contains the following statement:

> Most real homosexual prisoners have more than enough suitors to
> choose from. Contrary to popular myth, rarely do they solicit or
> attack other men. As long as a gay prisoner is quiet about his sexu-
> ality and only has a few partners, he is pretty much left alone.[16]

The Prison Rape Elimination Act was passed in 2003 through bipartisan cooperation in the U.S. Senate and House of Representatives. It promised to reduce rape in prison beginning with a thorough study of the problem, followed by recommendations for national standards "for enhancing the detection, prevention, reduction, and punishment of prison rape," as well as the treatment of rape victims. Grants from the government totaling $40 million dollars were approved for state and local governments to help limit the incidents of rape in prison. Those who are close observers of the prisons tell me that some progress has been made. Carolyn adds:

> 'Rape' is a rare incident around here. Sadly, participation in abusive
> relationships is consensual. Many of these women get involved in
> self-defeating connections with each other that mirror the similar-

16. Ross and Richards, *Behind Bars*, 87.

ly destructive relationships they have had with men on the outside,
and many times 'the abused' becomes 'the abuser.'

Self-inflicted injuries in jails and prisons occur as the result of over-crowded conditions, the oppressive weight of guilt, and, at times, because of segregation, (i.e., the practice of isolating individual offenders in cells for either punishment or protection). While cell protection is a welcome relief for those whose crimes might provoke attacks from other inmates, there are times when it becomes the breaking point of sanity. This is especially true when such isolation continues beyond a reasonable period of time without periodic reviews to determine whether or not the original reason for the segregation continues to exist.

BEING SICK IN PRISON

Prison is not the best place in the world to be sick. Certain living conditions in prison foster illnesses of various kinds. The constant noise, problems with food, presence of infectious organisms, and pervasiveness of despair all contribute to diseases of the mind and body. Serious illness or injury is dreaded because of the fear and uncertainty related to inadequate medical services. The competency of prison medical personnel is regularly questioned and the good people always seem to be stretched too far in serving the large prison population.

The best preventive health care in the prison is self-care. Sufficient exercise, carefully choosing what to eat from what is served, and taking all possible hygienic precautions are each important to maintaining good health. Family intervention, in cases of serious illness, sometimes helps to obtain the care needed to sustain life for a loved one in prison.

One of the greatest challenges to proper treatment of those in prison exists in the area of mental health. It is estimated that there are three times as many men and women with mental illness in U.S. prisons as there are in mental hospitals. If diagnostic services functioned at peak efficiency, there still would not be enough prison placement facilities to take care of them. Many of the mentally ill are in prison because they did not have access to treatment for their illnesses while they were on the outside.

JUVENILE OFFENDERS

Juvenile crime is a serious problem today. A history of neglect and abuse imposed on children by the adults in their lives often leads to rebelliousness and, subsequently, to acts of lawlessness associated with substance abuse. There are not enough safety nets in place to prevent youngsters left to fend for themselves from being lost each day to criminal activity. Neither are there enough concerned citizens who will speak out against the problem of disproportionately long prison sentences for crimes committed by youth under the age of eighteen.

Juveniles, upon being sentenced for criminal acts and put in jail, are susceptible to suicide attempts. This happens for different reasons, some of them stemming from the punishing conditions into which they have been placed. These conditions often spill over into correctional facilities where there is staff abuse as well as incidents of assault and rape among the inmates themselves. A striking difference is found in youth facilities operating in the state of Missouri where one-on-one attention is provided in residential treatment facilities and where, during the course of a three-year period, the re-incarceration rate has been less than 10 percent.

Missouri's good record in housing juvenile offenders stems from attention being paid to the provisions of the Juvenile Justice and Delinquency Prevention Act passed by Congress in 1974, the purpose of which was to decrease the abuses children suffered while incarcerated. It also speaks well of a state legislature that has continued to be conscious of how these young offenders need the kind of treatment offered by better-trained correctional personnel and the kind of environment that prevents the stigma of imprisonment to exert its negative influence.

John Huber's book *Last Chance in Texas: The Redemption of Criminal Youth* highlights a successful program for juvenile offenders at the Giddings State School in Texas. The Capital and Serious Violent Offenders Program serves teenage offenders whose crimes range from assault to murder. Participants in the program attend group therapy sessions where they share and work through the stories of their criminal violence. These encounters often lead to the release of repressed anger over having been abused as children. A 2004 study of those who successfully completed the Capital Offenders program at the Giddings State School revealed that thirty-six months after their release on parole, only ten percent had been re-arrested for a violent offense. Only three percent were re-arrested for violent crimes in the year following their release.[17]

News stories of physical abuse, including sexual assaults, in a West Texas youth facility appeared early in the year 2007, thereby placing the entire Texas Youth Commission under close scrutiny and pointing to serious problems in all of them. The head of the agency was fired and new leadership appointed. Staff members carrying felony offenses were automatically dismissed. Unfortunately, almost a year later, the omission of due process hearings and individual treatment plans as pointed out by an alert ombudsman has focused more negative attention upon the Texas Youth Commission. In assessing such unconscionable treatment of a vulnerable population it should not be forgotten that some employees in these facilities have rendered exceptional service in bringing wild and rebellious youth into a better way of thinking and acting.

WOMEN IN PRISON

The number of women in prison has multiplied during recent years. According to the National Institute of Justice, their numbers are growing at a rate almost twice that of men.

> ... excessive imprisonment has taken a particularly heavy toll on the approximately 3.2 million women per year who are arrested, charged with a (usually drug-related) crime, removed from their communities, and placed in jail to await trial or some other disposition of their case.[18]

An overwhelming majority of the women in prison today were poor, undereducated, and unemployed prior to their arrest and conviction. Many of them are mothers with children being taken care of by relatives or friends. While there is less evidence of physical violence among women than among men, which goes along with the fact that fewer women than men commit violent crimes, the stress level of women in prison is extremely high. Services specifically for women are either deficient or nonexistent.

The large number of women squeezed into spaces built for fewer numbers is excessively stressful and dangerous. An example of this is the Julia Tutwiler Prison for women in Wetumpka, Alabama. The prison was built in the early forties and was designed to hold 364 women. In 2002,

17. Huber, *Last Chance in Texas*, Introduction, *xxiii*.
18. Logan, *Good Punishment?*, 77.

the prison housed more than 1,000 women. The 91 assaults reported at Tutwiler in 2002 made this prison for women the most violent of all the prisons in the state of Alabama. The care received by the women at Tutwiler with mental illnesses and dangerous diseases was tragically inadequate and assaults took place with alarming frequency. Finally, suits were filed, first by prisoners asking for relief from the crowded conditions, and then by corrections officers, over unsafe working conditions. The state, without enough prison space anywhere to provide the needed relief, sent hundreds of women with the best records to a private prison in Louisiana. There they remain cooler, safer, and cleaner, but 500 miles away from their children and their families.[19]

A common tragedy related to women in prison is how many have been hurt by possessive and abusive men in their lives. In fact, there are women in prison who have been a party to criminal acts that they did not plan or that, in the company of a male companion, they did not anticipate. Those who find no other way out commit desperate acts in an attempt to rid themselves of a cruelly manipulative partner and end up in prison convicted of serious assault or murder. Women, seeking the kind of male attachment that offers them protection and security, frequently become victims of the kind of battering that should trigger an immediate exit strategy but all too often does not.

Advocates of women in prison have expressed concern that correctional officers are untrained in matters unique to incarcerated women. Actually, women employed by prison systems voice many of these same concerns. They wish to make prison less threatening to women, including the need to be protected from sexual exploitation. Many women who have been victims of abuse outside of prison continue to live with fear and disrespect inside of prison.

Women in prison are more disturbed than men by their loss of freedom to dress and act in harmony with their moods and desires. They are also more troubled over limited lines of communication with their loved ones. Their loss of privacy is upsetting and the body searches, to which they are regularly subjected, are a cause of emotional trauma and embarrassment. The understanding Marilyn and I gained of women in prison comes not only from what we learned from our daughter but from the two years we spent at the L. G. Plane State Jail as volunteer chaplains. Marilyn,

19. Gibbons and Katzenbach, "Confronting Confinement," 26. Gibbons and Katzenbach co-chair the Commission on Safety and Abuse in America's Prisons.

as a certified volunteer, was permitted to stay in a work room with the inmate clerks on the chaplain's morning off so they could complete their routine office work. At the same time, in an adjacent office, I counseled offenders who sent requests to the chaplain for a visit. The women were grateful to have the two of us there to assist them. We learned how impatiently many of them wait to receive letters from family members. They were particularly worried about how their children were doing and if, in serving time, they might lose custody of them.

One day, after considerable effort, I connected an offender by telephone with her young teenage son at a juvenile detention center in Beaumont. She had received word that her son had gotten into several fights. Listening to their conversation, I was impressed with how firm the mother was with her son and how he listened without objection to the advice she offered. That talk was not easy for her, but she did her best to bring him to his senses. After she hung up the phone, she cried . . . and I prayed.

CHILDREN OF THE INCARCERATED

Children of men and women in prison suffer in the saddest ways and, quite often, receive the least attention of those who are hurt by crime and its consequences of confinement and separation. We cannot forget the sight of small children being carried out of a visitation room while looking back and screaming, "Mommy, Mommy!" No one who appreciates the bond between a parent and a child can remain unmoved by innocent children who do not understand why their mother or father can't come home with them.

We believe that children should be taken to visit a mother or father in prison. They need times of being with the incarcerated parent in order to keep the connection as secure as possible. This is not as difficult when other lines of communication are kept open. If there is a reason for not visiting, there should be regular mail contacts that include whatever is part of the child's current training accomplishments. Such simple things as drawings or pages of coloring can be important. Hope for the future should not be abandoned if at all possible.

The stories told by Nell Bernstein in her excellent book *All Alone in the World: Children of the Incarcerated*, allow us to see prison through the eyes of children and to recognize the bitter price so many of them pay as the result of criminal punishment. She writes in the introduction to her book:

> These children have committed no crime, but the penalty they
> are forced to pay is steep. They forfeit, all too often, much of
> what matters to them: their home, their public status and private
> self-image, their primary source of comfort and affection. Their
> lives and prospects are profoundly affected by the numerous in-
> stitutions that lay claim to their parents—police, courts, jails and
> prisons, probation and parole—but they have no rights, explicit or
> implicit, within any of these jurisdictions. Conversely, there is no
> requirement that systems serving children—schools, child welfare
> departments, juvenile justice agencies—so much as take note of
> parental incarceration.[20]

The troubled lives of the children of prisoners is revealed in the
mental disturbances they suffer, the anxiety, the stress, and the breaking
up of families, as well as what so often follows—their own early entry into
criminal activity. Another weight many of these children carry includes
"the burden of being their absent parents' reason for living."[21]

The balanced perspective presented by Bernstein regarding the problems faced by children of incarcerated parents includes a statement that
sheds light on the broader issue of prison itself and how it has become
such a deeply rooted institution of American life.

> It is quite likely that the various adults this child will encounter
> along his route will make an effort to treat him kindly. The problem
> is not the callousness of individuals but the mechanical indiffer-
> ence of multiple bureaucracies, each of which functions according
> to its own imperatives. These bureaucratic exigencies—rather than
> children's experience—become the lens through which policies
> and protocols are drawn up and assessed. The system is viewed as
> 'working' when it works for the institutions that comprise it—in
> itself a legislative end. But when children's experience is not also
> given priority, the effect is to leave children feeling afraid, alone
> and unseen.[22]

Texas prisons allow eligible women offenders to have bonding visits
with their children who are fifteen years of age or under. The prison provides a private room for such visits and allows several hours of holding,
playing, and visiting. This helps to maintain a valuable closeness between
these mothers and their children. Children in Texas between 10 and

20. Bernstein, *All Alone in the World*, 4.

21. Ibid., 50.

22. Ibid., 11–12.

15 years of age who have a parent incarcerated in a county jail or state or federal prison can enroll, at no charge, in a special camp sponsored by the Episcopal Diocese of Texas. Camp Good News is held at Camp Allen, near Navasota, Texas, on beautiful acreage owned by the Diocese. It features spiritual activities of prayer, praise, and worship, along with the more physical challenges of swimming, horseback riding, games, crafts, and skills growth. The camp, coordinated by Ed Davis and carried out by a staff of dedicated volunteers, can accommodate 60 boys and girls, (first come, first served) where children can experience the unconditional love of God within a community of caring people.

CORRECTIONAL OFFICERS

The official title of prison employees responsible for security, and who have custodial and supervisory authority over prisoners, is "correctional officer." People on the outside commonly refer to them as "guards." These men and women have the unenviable task of keeping order in the prison while maintaining their own composure in the face of taunts, insults, and bribe attempts. They are expected to be distant and dismissive toward offenders, and never to display softness, especially within sight of ranking officers. They are cautioned to be alert for trouble before it develops and to strictly enforce prison rules. While some correctional officers are able, in small ways, to contribute something positive to the lives of offenders, many have personal problems along with the difficulties of environmental stress. Low pay, relational conflicts, and burnout all take their toll.

Convicts who have grown wiser through their years in prison are most often able to maintain their composure in the face of insults and demeaning treatment by correctional officers. Jorge Antonio Renaud offers an interesting perspective on this subject:

> In my opinion many disciplinary cases arise from situations where an officer harasses an inmate and the inmate refuses to give in, out of pride, or anger, or peer pressure, or sometimes just stupidity. Inmates know that some officers will take any opportunity to exercise their authority. None of this wounds us or makes us bleed, or does anything other than hurt our prison pride, or our false dignity, something we need to discard and replace with a sense of responsibility for our actions.[23]

23. Renaud, *Behind the Walls*, 112–13.

The correctional officers with whom we have had the most frequent contact regularly display courtesy and a willingness to assist us. On the other hand, we do not fully appreciate the difficulties they encounter in their day-to-day contact with offenders. We can only imagine how much their tolerance level is lowered as they work under conditions that cause them to become upset, angry, and agitated.

FEDERAL PRISONS

I met a man one day who was waiting to visit a friend at the L. G. Plane State Jail for women near Dayton, Texas. He said he once worked as a prison guard at the federal prison in Leavenworth, Kansas, and went on to tell me about the wall of fame that features large pictures of celebrities, the majority of them entertainers, who served time at the Leavenworth Federal Penitentiary. I asked him if that area of the prison is open to the public and he replied, "Oh yes, visitors come in there all the time."

The enactment of mandatory sentencing laws for drug and drug-related crimes under federal jurisdiction, beginning in 1984, caused a dramatic increase in the federal prison population. These mandatory sentences effectively took away the authority federal judges had to extend leniency in clearly warranted circumstances. Many federal judges complained that their responsibilities were reduced to those of clerks and computers. In addition, as the number of federal prisoners increased, the building of new prisons became necessary. There is hope at this time for returning some of the more important aspects of federal crime sentencing to the judges.

At the turn of the century, there was a major focus on crimes of corporate greed. Executives have been caught in schemes that resulted in both shareholders and company employees being hurt. Many of these crimes resulted in federal sentences of substantial duration. The so-called "white collar" criminals feel the weight of prison life in ways that are frightening to them or at least unpleasantly demeaning. They share the company of drug dealers, petty thieves, forgers, and those who have engaged in child pornography.

Federal prisoners are issued khaki clothing and are allowed very little personal property. Specifically, they are allowed one religious text, one pair of glasses (but no contact lenses), dentures, a wedding ring with no stones, $20.00 in change for vending machines, and a commissary account. Most of the federal prisoners are required to work in jobs that pay between 12 cents and 40 cents an hour. Living conditions are tight. Bunk beds are crammed into small cubicles that hold two to six inmates with newcomers getting the top bunk. Federal prison inmates who are approved for visitation may receive visitors on Sunday, Monday, Thursday, Friday, and Saturday, as well as holidays, from 8:30 a.m. to 3:00 p.m. In addition, inmates who have available cash on record can make monitored telephone calls, up to 300 minutes per month, to those who have been approved to receive such calls.

PRIVATE PRISONS

Private prisons take care of only a small percentage of the nation's prison population. There were, in 2007, just over 140,000 beds under private company control. Some of these companies have been particularly successful in competing for contracts with local, state, and federal jurisdictions. The location of private prisons where access to employees is available and the land is reasonably priced helps them to secure a favorable market position. Inmates housed in private prisons, along with their supporters, argue that these corporate entities do not support crime prevention measures or classes in prison related to the re-integration of offenders into society.

Private prisons, in addition to easing the intake load of states with high prisoner population totals, accept offenders from other states where overcrowding is a problem. For example, in 2007, the Harris County Jail sent 400 inmates carrying minor offenses to a private prison in Louisiana. The overcrowding of prisons will likely result in the continuing transfer of prisoners away from the areas most convenient for the visitation of their family members and friends.

An investigation into the suicide of an Idaho prisoner who was transferred to a private company's Texas prison revealed two serious problems with private prisons. One problem occurs when states having jurisdiction over prisoners sent to another state do not hold the private prison accountable through regular inspections for how their prisoners are treated. The other problem, occurring too frequently, is when excessive "bottom line" interests contribute to sub-standard living conditions and limit restorative programs for offenders.

The leaders of Presbyterian and Catholic churches have questioned private prisons on moral grounds. They have expressed concern over whether prisons operating for a profit can realistically offer programs that will help offenders stay out of prison when they are released. In addition, they support the argument that cutting expenses, increasing prison populations, and lengthening sentences are tied to a political agenda of those who stand to gain in a variety of ways from having a private prison in their district.

PRISON TIME LOSSES

Men and women who experience the loss of family members and friends while doing their time in prison are largely unnoticed by the free-world population. Many prisoners have family members who, as they grow older, become unable to visit as frequently. Other relationships are lost through the passage of time. Prisoners receive news about family members who are retiring from their employment. They receive news about a death in the family and realize with sadness that they are not eligible to attend the funeral. Brothers and sisters get married and establish families of their own even as personal thoughts of going home become lost in the rushing tide of time. Some long-term convicts no longer receive visits or mail. Lennie Spitale, who spent several years in prison, writes about the sadness of a family lost through time. He describes the large piece of poster board dominating the central portion of the wall opposite another inmate's bunk.

> This was his life staring back at him, or at least the sacred part of it. Like faces forever frozen in some mysterious time warp, they existed only in a lost and faraway country, a fantasy world like the Land of Oz. This world did exist once, and, in the man's memories it still did. That poster was holy ground. I couldn't imagine how many times his eyes had come to rest upon the citizens of that other world as he lay there in an arrested state of metamorphosis, trapped in the cocoon of his own reality.[24]

Philip Brasfield, a Texas convict currently in his thirty-first year of prison time, writing in response to my request, shares feelings about his mother's death and the continuing influence of her life upon his.

> Because I had once been a part of her, because God had knit me inside her womb, I was closer to her than any other living person. It was Mama I knew longest and who knew me the best and I relied on that mutual knowledge and intimacy as if it was the solid rock of my foundation. The disease of Alzheimer's fractured that rock, at first gradually, then more and more rapidly until the person I knew

24. Spitale, *Prison Ministry*, 113. Used by permission.

as my mother became estranged by undeniable fragmentation of cognition, her memory of time, place, self and others, and in the end, the very notion of her own existence. After she mercifully died and was buried, my grief and sense of loss kept me blinded to the reality of her life imprinting mine in so many ways. So I reverted to my own earliest memories of her at my bedside, reciting the Rosary as I lay in a fever, or sitting beside my bed late at night teaching me the prayers that continue to sustain me to this day. Simply, I prayed that God's mercy and compassion would welcome her to an eternal life devoid of the worries and fears, the vagaries of human failings, and the disappointments life handed my mother during her 85 years on this earth. After a time, my sense of loss became lessened by a feeling that she had indeed 'gone home' and would be waiting for me to get there some day, too.

The losses experienced by serving time in prison are impossible to imagine by those who live in the comfort and security of the outside world. And yet, in the midst of such sorrow and deprivation, there are signs not only of survival but of hope. Cries from the depths of need reach the heart of God whose attentiveness to the marginalized includes the prisoners and those who care for them.

HOW PRISON LOSES ITS POWER

Remember Jesus Christ, raised from the dead, a descendant of David, that is my gospel, for which I suffer hardship, even to the point of being chained like a criminal; but the word of God is not chained.

—2 Timothy 2:8–9

Prison loses its power when prisoners are moved by the spiritual gifts of unchained melodies. The good news of God's redeeming work is sung in Charles Wesley's triumphant hymn, "O, for a Thousand Tongues to Sing." It affirms that "He breaks the power of canceled sin, He sets the prisoner free . . ." Walter Brueggemann has suggested that "this God is oddly and characteristically attentive to the cry of the bondaged who find enough voice to risk self-announcement, that is, who become agents of their own history."[25]

---

25. Brueggemann, *Texts That Linger, Words That Explode*, 97.

Many of those who become free within the physical confinement of prison are given ways to enrich the fallow ground of prison life and reduce the capacity of incarceration to rob them of dignity and self-respect. The freedom possessed in Jesus' name finds allies in a variety of creative forms of literary and dramatic expression that from time to time slip into the prison. Grady Hillman II has more than twenty-five years of experience teaching creative writing and conducting arts-in-the-prisons programs in correctional facilities. In an interview that appeared in the "Zest" section of the Houston Chronicle on March 19, 2006, he provides insight into how negative prison behavior can be altered.

> In the depressing environment of prison, creating a piece of art, whether it's dance or music or creative writing, is connecting the internal world to an external reality and trying to communicate. The prisoners get very engaged in this process, and it's therapeutic, even if they're writing about anger or bitterness. For a while, they're transcending it . . .[26]

The writing of prisoners, such as that contained in the collection of H. Bruce Franklin, *Prison Writing in 20th Century America*, reveals how the prison experience can generate amazing stories. I made use of a very special prison incident contained in the book to illustrate a Christmas sermon, "Love Came Down at Christmas." The story, written by Donald Lowrie from his book *My Life in Prison*, explained how John Hoyle, a new warden at San Quentin, was able to stop the traditional New Year's Eve rioting by surprising the prisoners with an unusual Christmas morning kindness. On Christmas Eve, according to the story, the warden made rounds and saw empty socks hanging outside each cell. Such action, in remembrance of what they did as children, touched him deeply. He sent an officer into San Quentin Point to buy up all the candy he could find and stuff the stockings that always before had remained empty. On New Year's Eve of 1907, instead of the raucous noise of rioting and the destruction of prison property, not a sound was heard from the cell blocks of San Quentin Prison.

Poetry often takes root and grows in places of restricted movement. As a result, prison poetry deserves close attention. As a craft that helps to resist boredom and the feeling of being trapped by uselessness, poetic forms of self-expression convey, with power and poignancy, a way prison-

26. Noted by permission of Grady Hillman II.

ers are able to be *in* but not *of* the strange land they occupy. Much of the poetry written in prison provides a mirror through which the incarcerated are able catch a glimpse of respectability. Prison poets are able to illustrate their time-bound circumstances with fiercely passionate verse. Some of their best poems support a prison survival strategy. Others reflect a cool detachment, a dream-like separation from the daily monotony of prison life. Included in winding passages of free verse are frozen images of the once familiar land from which the prisoner came, as well as a visionary projection of the land to which he or she hopes one day to return. As a language of subversion, prison poetry defies the powers, offering the promise of deliverance within an imaginative reconstruction of the way out of Babylon.

Prisoners do not become poets simply by being incarcerated. Only a few, endowed with the potential for expressing themselves in this special way, are able to break out of the cocoon they occupy with words that dip and soar like newly released butterflies. Within their world of fear and degradation, with its constant reminders of thrown away lives, the prison poets work to perfect their craft, boldly resisting the dying of the light. They employ a language often purchased, with words I borrow from William Butler Yeats, "in the foul rag and bone-shop of the heart."

Bedford Hills Correctional Facility for Women in Westchester County, New York, features a writing class for women, most of whom committed murder, called "What I Want My Words To Do To You." Fifteen women at one time study under playwright and activist Eve Ensler. She helps the women tell the stories of their heart-wrenching personal journeys through life that go deep into the causes, details, and consequences of their crimes. The noted actress Glenn Close has endorsed the results of this intense and personal writing project.

Prison art becomes a way for certain prisoners to be recognized in a special way, even though a common perception of prison art is that it is bizarre and offensive. Accomplished prison artists are sometimes allowed to market their craft in the outside world. One artist at Pelican Bay State Prison in California was disciplined for what a prison rule defines as "engaging in a revenue generating or profit making activity." This artist, located in solitary confinement, paints with a brush he created out of his own hair. He turns the colors from M & M's into a kind of paint and separates them into plastic containers that held grape jelly. Postcards are used for canvases. The objection to the disciplinary action taken against him is that he had donated his art to the Pelican Bay Prison Project, a charity that promised to honor the prisoner's request that the proceeds from the sale ($500 for each painting) would be used to help the children of prisoners.

United Methodist Bishop Kenneth L. Carder writes about a relationship he established with jail inmates that led to his idea that the talent some of them possessed for creating cartoon drawings could be directed to a special purpose.

> Several men who occupied the same cellblock in one county jail were particularly adept at creating cartoons. I provided them with copies of the New Testament in a modern translation and asked them to read the parables and sayings of Jesus and identify those that lent themselves to cartoon portrayal. The result was a collection of insightful portrayals of the blind leading the blind, a rich man trying to go through the eye of a needle, a man removing the speck from another's eye while a log was protruding from his own, and the laying up of treasures where moth and rust destroy and thieves steal. The cartoons led to long hours of discussion of the teachings of Jesus that would rival most seminary classes for passion and depth of insight.[27]

Marilyn and I were moved by the art of juvenile offenders whose work was displayed at St. Luke's United Methodist Church. The display sponsor, the Children's Prison Arts Project, provides juvenile offenders with classes that lead to artistic expressions of the life they experience. The tears, for example, drawn with bold strokes on many of their paintings, are obvious signs of the pain they need to release in order to open their lives to the gift of healing.

Drama instruction in prison can also bring healing, as witnessed in "Shakespeare Behind Bars" which was featured on CNN news on February 13, 2003. Prisoners in the Luther Lockett Correctional Facility in Louisville, Kentucky present *dramatis personae* in instructive performances of Shakespeare. An amazing teacher leads offenders through the dramas of life as written by the great bard. In reading the lines of Shakespeare's characters, actors on the prison stage come to a better understanding of themselves. The instructor insists that these men are not stupid. He does not condone their past actions but he supports, as does

---

27. Carder, ". . . You Visited Me: The Call to Prison Ministry," 28. Copyright © 2006 Christian Century. Reprinted by permission.

the warden of the facility, the premise that those who have gone through the acting experience will not be as likely to return to prison.

"The Prison Show," hosted by Ray Hill, an ex-convict and political activist, reaches out with messages to prisoners in Texas through radio station KPFT-FM in Houston. Every Friday evening his program goes out to prisoners within broadcast range who have access to a radio. Family members and friends are a part of the listening audience. Various subjects related to prison life are presented by regular and special guests on the show. Quite often, mailing addresses are provided so that inmates may write for information that is helpful in reviewing sentencing options, similar cases, and parole guidelines. Offenders throughout the state are familiar with Ray Hill's work and write to him with questions. He responds with letters that provide the best answers to the problems they are facing.

The second hour of the show consists of calls from family members and friends to loved ones in prison who are able to catch the broadcast. This hour of many one-way conversations is filled with expressions of love, concern, advice, and encouragement. Two recorded songs, one played at the beginning of the program and the other played at the end, hauntingly depict what many family members feel as they support loved ones in prison. The last song, called "The Prison Show with Ray," written and sung by Gerald Bates, came from an evening when Gerald accidentally picked up Ray's show on his car radio. He was so impressed by several of the messages callers were conveying to relatives in prison that he drove into a parking lot and wrote the song.

Texas' Death Row is home for a young man who I visit as a Spiritual Adviser (the prison designation of anyone qualified to represent a particular denomination or faith to offenders). One day, I received a letter from him in which he asked if I had ever heard J. S. Bach's "Sheep May Safely Graze." He added, "The best way I can describe that music is that it is angelic." His comment reminded me of how faith is so beautifully expressed through music and of how, even in the shadow of death, there are moments when a heavenly song steals upon the ear of the most earthly deprived. Unfortunately, those who live too comfortably often miss the music that comforts, inspires and, in mysterious ways, sends us forth as messengers to the dying.

The songs of prisoners are a threat to the power of the prison. Singing offers a passionate resistance to hopelessness. When gifts of wonder, love, and praise break into prison on the wings of a song, "help for today and bright hope for tomorrow"[28] becomes a prison possibility and many of those who never learned to sing are found auditioning for the choir.

"Hail to the Lord's Anointed" is a beautiful Advent hymn based on Psalm 72. It was written by James Montgomery (1771–1854), a newspaper editor and social justice advocate in England, who wrote poetry while serving time in prison for his radical views. The text reminds us of the purpose of "Great David's greater Son" to deliver the poor and needy from oppression and violence. An unmistakable clue to God's justice initiative on behalf of prisoners who suffer wrong is revealed in the last two lines of the second stanza:

> To give them songs for sighing, their darkness turned to light;
> Whose souls, condemned and dying, are precious in his sight.

Snow at the Ramsey I Trusty Camp in Southeast Texas on Christmas Eve, 2004, forced the oppressive authority of the prison to be temporarily suspended. This unusual accumulation of snow on the ground attracted a lot of attention. The letter I received from my friend David, who lived there at the time, described it:

> What a Christmas! I don't know what it was like in the city (Houston), but here we got 13 inches of snow beginning Christmas Eve afternoon and continuing throughout the night. Most of us had never seen so much snow. The whole trusty camp turned into a bunch of little boys, building snow men, snow forts, and having snowball wars. My friend M___ said he believed it was a miracle from God—that just some snow falling on Christmas abolished all our prejudices and hatreds and we all became one big family, having fun and forgetting our differences on the day we celebrate Christ's birth. He was right, I have never seen prisoners get along so well in my life . . .

SUMMARY CONCLUSIONS

Prisons contain those who, because of the crimes they have committed, must bear the pain of incarceration apart from the customs of life the majority of us take for granted. They also contain many who have only

---

28. From the hymn, "Great is Thy Faithfulness," written by Thomas O. Chisholm.

hurt themselves and who need considerate guidance back into the world outside of prison. Prisons make it hard for those who live inside them for any length of time to be accepted for reasons that relate to the mercy of love and forgiveness.

While we too often presume that prison is the last line of defense against lawlessness, what slips by unpublicized is the extent to which prison has become a major training ground for lawlessness. Meanwhile, an uncaring majority carries out the "rush to riches" agenda of prison growth business interests. Suppliers of all manner of security equipment, such as weapons, riot gear, and locking devices, along with uniforms, food, medical supplies, and office equipment, make their sales pitches to system officials in charge of purchasing. On the other hand, in spite of the reasons to believe how seriously prisons are failing all of us, there are ways through which goodness and mercy enter the lives of imprisoned men and women and sets them on higher ground.

One of the strongest messages in the Bible teaches how easy it is for us to ignore the very ones through whose eyes Jesus pleads for our help. This is the precise point at which the church is called to inform, enlist, and empower its members in ministry to prisoners. Through every effort to understand and respond to the various crises caused by crime, including how prisons drain financial and human resources, there is the constant challenge to proclaim the freedom in Christ whereby the power of the prison is overcome. This, of course, is a freedom that does not depend upon all of the problems of the prison being solved. In fact, "because they (prisoners) understand the political reality of their lives, they grasp more easily the truth that without an alternative community that rightly challenges the powers with the truth of the Gospel, there can be no hope."[29]

29. Hauerwas, *Dispatches from the Front*, 113.

5

The Texas Prison System

Ain't no more cane on the Brazos,
Cause we done ground it all to molasses.[1]

—Author Unknown

TEXAS IS A LAW and order state. Legislators and a majority of the voting public do everything possible to keep it that way. The early Texas tradition of hanging horse thieves has simply moved into a system of justice that moves a lot slower and punishes in a wider variety of ways.

A BRIEF HISTORY

The town of Huntsville, located in the piney woods of East Texas, became the home of the Texas State Penitentiary in 1846. The famous "Walls" prison (known officially as the Huntsville Unit) was built in 1849. Located near the town square and only a few blocks from Sam Houston State University, it is clearly identified by its red brick walls. These walls, beginning in 1923, enclosed the location where electric chair executions were carried out in Texas. A total of 361 men met their death while strapped down in "Old Sparky." Famous guests of this Huntsville prison include John Wesley Hardin and Clyde Barrow along with the musician Hudie Leadbetter, better known as "Leadbelly." The total number of convicts in the state penitentiary in 1866 was 264.

The Wynne Unit, in the town of Huntsville, started out as Texas' first prison farm. It began operations in 1883 on 1,900 acres where vegetable crops were grown to help provide food for the Huntsville convicts. Many

---

1. Words from a prison work song. The Brazos River runs past many of the old prison farms in Texas.

people still call it the "Wynne Farm." A few years later, the state started buying up large segments of land in various areas of East Texas that became prison farms. By 1921 these prison farms encompassed more than 81,000 acres.

A number of Texas prisoners, during the days following the Civil War, brought songs of the plantation with them to the vast acreage of the prison farms. Some of these songs persisted in various forms into the latter part of the twentieth century. A man by the name of Bruce Jackson put together a collection of prison songs in a book called *Wake Up Dead Man: Afro-American Worksongs from Texas Prisons*. The music, as an exclusive property of the slave/convicts, kept them going in the fields from sunrise to sunset. It enabled them to help one another and to create a lyric consciousness of self-worth that future generations would be able to claim for themselves in a variety of ways.

The treatment of prisoners in Texas during the early days was particularly brutal. Between 1867 and 1912, the state dealt with overcrowding by leasing convicts for labor purposes to private industry with the money going into the state treasury. The results of a survey conducted by the Texas Commission on Prisons and Prison Labor in 1924 reported that "Texas needs new methods of dealing with her prisoners . . . (and) new methods for training them." It went on to report that "the majority of the prisoners suffered from mental and physical deficiencies and had not completed primary school."[2]

The Goree Unit, built in Huntsville in 1907, became the first prison in the state for women in 1910. In the 1980's, Goree became a male facility and the Texas Department of Corrections transferred the women prisoners to facilities formerly utilized by the Texas Youth Council near Gatesville in Coryell County. Goree now shares intake duties with the nearby Byrd Unit with assignments of longer duration being made after the process has been completed. Female offenders, bound for medical treatment in Galveston or permanent unit assignments, are sometimes housed overnight at Goree.

When the Texas prison population of the 1980s began to overflow the existing prisons, a large number of offenders were released. This brought forth wild and fearful demands from the public to do something. The state legislature's answer was a prison building boom that more than

2. *Handbook of Texas Online*, http://www.tshaonline.org/handbook/online/articles/TT/mdtva.html, lines 86–91.

tripled the prison population. A majority of the newer Texas prisons were located in rural areas where the potential for prison employees was readily available and the local citizens could feel good about such a significant boost to their economy. Tax breaks, job training, and a variety of incentives had towns competing for a prison.

The Texas Prison Board became the Texas Board of Corrections in 1957. In 1960, the Huntsville Penitentiary and the prison farms were designated as "Units." In 1989 the state legislature abolished the Texas Board of Corrections, the Board of Pardons and Paroles, and the Adult Probation Commission, and merged them into the Texas Department of Criminal Justice (TDCJ). A new Correctional Institution Division was formed in 2003 that divided 112 prison facilities, including private prisons, into seven regions in Texas.

The Texas Department of Criminal Justice had 155,651 offenders in prisons across the state as of February 29, 2008.[3] Huntsville, along with being the headquarters for the Texas Prison System, is also the location where more than 9,000 state prisoners are housed within five facilities located inside the city limits, with two other prisons not far out of town housing approximately 5,600 people.

Restorative justice advocates and other concerned citizens mounted a serious lobbying effort in 2007 that focused on urging state legislators to reject a proposal to build more prisons. A determined counter-offensive by supporters of additional prison beds secured a last minute vote to allow the Texas Department of Criminal Justice to petition the Legislative Budget Board for approval to float bonds to build 3 to 6 new facilities. On a more positive note, an approval vote was obtained to restore 5,000 treatment beds for state jail substance abuse treatment programs. In addition, funding for drug court programs statewide was approved along with several other measures, including the restoration of 21 chaplain positions.

LIFE IN TEXAS PRISONS

Texas inmates feel invisible. They feel that nothing they do is recognized. It is but one step from that to agreeing, subconsciously but sincerely, that if the others who dress like them, look like them and act like them, are guilty and worthy of punishment, so are they.[4]

3. Information supplied by Alicia Frezia-King, Open Records Act Coordinator, TDCJ Executive Services.

4. Renaud, *Behind the Walls*, 19.

The majority of first-time offenders begin their experience with the Texas Prison System at one of several diagnostic units across the state. Prison personnel in these facilities have the responsibility to obtain from each new state prisoner a wide range of personal information that includes the type of conviction and the amount of time set as punishment. All of this falls under the broad heading of "classification." Classification determines a security level that, in turn, leads to a custody designation of minimum, medium, close, or maximum supervision. Factors involved are age, type of offense, and county jail behavior. A thorough psychological testing process completes each offender profile.

Texas prison life is introduced to many first-offense newcomers through outside work designed to test their mettle. Subsequently, this familiar form of field labor, known as "hoe squad" duty, may be assigned as a disciplinary action. Hoe squads, often seen from roads near the prisons, consist of teams of fifteen to thirty inmates who perform field work. Correctional officers, usually on horseback, watch over each team. Travelers along the roads bordering prison land are able to see offenders lifting their hoes high in the air and then sending them crashing to the ground. At times, from the depths of these convicted souls, there emerges a rhythmic chant carrying a lonely cry of release. Under the hot Texas sun, the prison fields become, through these rituals of bondage, places of spiritual freedom.

Offender jobs are assigned on the basis of classification, experience, and unit needs. Everyone involved with Texas prisons acknowledges that inmates are given major responsibilities in performing the work that keeps the prisons running. There are very few jobs that inmates are not allowed to perform in prison, but certain jobs require a minimum custody status and a clear disciplinary record. While inmate work is generally supervised, the supervisors themselves often learn details of the job from the inmates.

Time spent in a Texas prison includes working, eating, and sleeping. It also includes, in varying degrees, physical exercise, reading, educational opportunities, law library work, and writing letters. Television and day room games provide a fairly large segment of time along with the greater reward of weekend visitation time and chapel services. When an inmate needs to visit with a unit official, including the chaplain, a form called an I-60 must be submitted requesting such a visit. Disciplinary action may be administered if an inmate leaves his or her living quarters without a form of approval in hand, or without being in the company of a correctional officer.

Offenders usually eat whenever their living area is summoned. Breakfast extends from 3:00 a.m. to 5:00 a.m., lunch from 9:30 a.m. to 12:30 p.m., and supper from 3:45 p.m. until 6:00 p.m. Lines of white-clad prison inmates, with eating on their minds, wind through the prison yard while being watched by a few gray-clad officers. A small window of time is available for sitting down and eating after prisoners enter the chow hall.

Indigent offenders are provided with the barest necessities and are denied many of the things most of us would consider essential to daily living. Prisoners are considered indigent who do not have funds available to them in an inmate trust fund established for them by family members or friends. The prison system allows indigent offenders to mail five first class letters per week without requiring reimbursement for postage, unless they have money put in their account within sixty days. The same provision applies to the few toiletry items they are given. Non-indigent offenders in jails and prisons must buy their own stamps and toiletry items.

Some of the sharpest dealers of goods and services within the prison population develop and refine schemes called "hustles" to tap the prison exchange market for desirable merchandise. Cigarettes are in great demand and drugs, though much harder to obtain, are known to be smuggled into prison through various means. While it may seem strange to hear about gambling, extortion, and a black market enterprise within prisons, such activities go hand in hand with internal theft and inmates being "called out" by other inmates as a means of "taking care of business." Correctional officers, meanwhile, weigh what they know and see, and make intervention decisions based on a largely subjective evaluation of the situation and the particular offenders involved.

Family members and friends can report problems a loved one is having in prison to the Ombudsman. A wide range of complaints and questions are taken every day. Quite a few of these complaints are about injuries inflicted upon a loved one by an officer or another offender. There are also reports of thefts of property and of excessive harassment. A good faith effort is generally put forth to find out what really happened and report back to the caller. Sometimes the reply is delayed because of complications related to "obtaining the facts."

Job training opportunities for Texas offenders is provided by Texas Correctional Industries. This program has forty-two manufacturing operations located at certain prisons that produce textiles, clothing, cleaning equipment, license plates, and furniture. The Agribusiness, Land and Minerals Division, puts offenders to work in packing plants, feed mills, and pest control. Quite a few jobs are available in machine repair, welding, veterinary services, and clerical services. The Facilities Division uses offenders in construction and building maintenance.

The Prison Industry Enhancement Program (PIE) enables certain prison inmates to work in manufacturing jobs in which they get paid slightly above minimum wage. Companies that apply for prison labor are required to have an operation outside of prison. This is the only prison labor program that pays for the work done by prisoners in Texas (about 500 of them in 2006), even though they only get to keep about 20 percent of it. The main portion goes to the state for room and board. Smaller percentages go to the offender's family and to crime victim restitution.

The Victim Services Division of the Texas Department of Criminal Justice provides special services to crime victims and their family members. A caring spirit accompanies the help provided in determining inmate status and the notification of victims about an inmate's release. In addition, assistance is provided in scheduling meetings with parole board members during parole reviews and processing the restitution due as part of a releasee's obligation to the actual victim of an offense. The division helps prepare a victim impact statement for use during the punishment phase of a jury's obligation and assists victims who wish to participate in a Victim Offender Mediation/Dialogue. Some offenders are brought to the point of accepting responsibility, as well as expressing remorse, for the crimes they committed.

The violation of a Texas prison rule for inmates results, most often, in a "case" (like a traffic ticket in the free world) being written by the investigating officer. This is followed by an appearance of the offender before the Unit Disciplinary Committee where the punishment is decided based on the seriousness of the offense. There may be a loss of weekend visitation rights, recreation time, commissary visits, and chapel attendance, or simply one or a combination of several of these privileges. There is also the possibility of serving time in solitary confinement for serious offenses such as possession of contraband, stealing or destroying state property, and sexual misconduct.

Administrative Segregation, commonly called "Ad-Seg," is the relocation of offenders into single cells for the purpose of maintaining safety, security, and order within the prison. Sometimes this alternative is used for the protection of a particular inmate whose life may have been threatened by other inmates. The unit warden may agree to an inmate's request to be placed in this protective form of custody.

Lockdowns constitute one of the most common sources of inmate complaints. They take place as a disciplinary response to widespread misbehavior or as a periodic control mechanism. During a lockdown offenders are given, for example, peanut butter and jelly sandwiches (sometimes bologna) called "johnnies" along with a piece of cake and, at times, some raisins. An additional problem associated with lockdowns occurs when visitation is cancelled and trips to the commissary are denied. Such a deprivation of privilege occurred in all of the Texas prisons when visitation was not allowed from late October to mid-November of 2008, resulting from a forbidden cell phone being used by an offender on Death Row. Intensive investigations in all of the prisons turned up some additional cell phones, causing grief for prison personnel as well as prison inmates.

Shakedowns are often a part of lockdowns. These extensive inspections of prisoner space (referred to by prisoners as their "house") can occur at any time and result in a chaos of confusion and irritation. Offenders pile all of their belongings on a sheet and then carry or drag it to a central location. There, correctional officers conduct a search for items that are illegal for offenders to have among their meager possessions.

I received a letter from Philip Brasfield, written during a lockdown where he lives at the Hughes Unit. I was moved by the fact that, after mentioning the "terrible rations," he marked the spot with an asterisk and at the bottom of the page wrote:

> I am palpably aware that our meager fare twice a year would be a boon and a feast to billions of others in the world. We are blessed therefore, even in prison, and even during such uncomfortable times as the present.

HEALTH CARE

The health care of Texas prisoners is managed by a nine-member Health Advisory Committee, with the day-to-day medical services handled by two health care systems: The University of Texas Medical Branch (UTMB) in Galveston and Texas Tech Health Science Center in Lubbock. An official statement from TDCJ instructs offenders how to report the need for medical treatment and directs them to fill out a sick call request (HSA-9) and drop it in a sick call request box. When offenders feel as if the medical treatment they have received is inadequate, they are advised to send an I-60 form (Inmate Request to Official) to the facility Manager of Health Care Services. An additional review, if desired, can be requested by writing to TDCJ's Patient Liaison Program.

There are no greater concerns of family members for their loved ones in prison than those associated with health care. There is very little relief for caring loved ones who must contend with the fear and uncertainty of a serious illness and the inadequacy of medical services for the one in prison whose life is precious to them. A frequent complaint about prison health care involves poor medical treatment by medical personnel. In addition, I am told that prison clinics often do not have enough supplies and a doctor is not always available.

Texas prisoners are not ordinarily allowed to keep containers of medication in their cells or dormitories. As a result, they are often found standing in "pill lines" to receive individual doses of their prescribed medication.

Texas convict Sheldon W. DeLuca tells a story of how bad it can be when hospital medical service is needed.[5]

> I had to go to the hospital last week. Do you remember the last time you made a trip to the hospital? First off, I had to pack up all my belongings and prepare to vacate my residence. That is standard procedure on this unit. Even if a 'resident' is only going to be away for one night, he must abandon his quarters. That's not the rule on all units, but it is probably the case for most of them. After packing all my belongings, as instructed, I took them out to the day room (just outside my cell). An officer ordered me to unpack everything so he could inventory all my belongings, then repack them to be taken to the property room for storage while I was gone.
>
> The following morning, I was awakened at five a.m. I had to take all my bedding—mattress, pillow, sheets, and blankets—to the laundry. After this, all of us who were going on the "chain bus" that morning were led outside where we were strip-searched. The temperature outdoors was about forty degrees that morning.
>
> Fortunately, due to a grievance other inmates had filed, we were allowed to keep our jackets (after being stripped naked) until the bus arrived. We were kept in a caged outdoor area near the back

5. Reprinted here by permission of DeLuca and the Texas Inmate Families Association, as published in the January/February 2003 edition of its newsletter, *TIFA Contact*.

gate until the bus got there, about 8:30 a.m.—more than three hours of waiting in the cold. We boarded the bus and headed for Huntsville, arriving at the Estelle II Unit about an hour later.

We stayed at Estelle through the weekend, then continued our trip to John Sealy Hospital in Galveston on Monday morning. When we arrived at Estelle we were given lunch and assigned to cells. We were each given two sheets but no pillow and no blankets. The nighttime temperature hovered around 40 degrees outside; inside the building (cell areas are not heated), it probably didn't cross 60. The inmates who are 'permanently' assigned to the unit get two blankets, but we had to sleep in our outer clothes in an attempt to stay warm. Bear in mind that I and the other inmates were being transported to a hospital for medical services.

Apparently no effort is made to keep the medical transfer cells at Estelle clean and sanitary. Food stains are on the bars, walls, and floors. Breakfast is served in the cells (at 12:30 a.m.); lunch and dinner are eaten in the cafeteria. One cell I stayed in had black mold growing in the corners. The inmates in these cells are locked down around the clock except for time to eat and shower, about an hour altogether. They are not allowed to bring books (even a Bible) or other reading material.

On Monday morning we were called out at 2:00 a.m. for the bus to take us the rest of the journey. The rationale for serving breakfast at 12:30 a.m. is to insure that the inmates eat before they leave, but in fact the bus didn't come at two o'clock; ours came at about 7:00 a.m. By nine o'clock, we were pulling into John Sealy Hospital, the main medical facility for most of TDCJ, operated by the University of Texas Medical Branch in Galveston. After intake processing, a nurse took my vital signs and I was ushered into an examining room. A few minutes later, a physician came in, introduced himself as a surgical resident, and asked what my problem was. I told him that I have a hernia (and have had it for about eighteen months). He asked to see it, and said, 'That's a hernia, all right. We can fix you up.' Then he left. A few minutes later, a nurse came in and said, 'We'll have to re-schedule you to come back down here for your surgery.'

When I pointed out that this was my second trip to Sealy for this surgery in as many months, she said, 'This is a busy hospital. You might have to come down here three or four times before we can get you in for your operation.'

EDUCATION

Eligible Texas offenders may benefit from a statewide program of education under the Windham School District. The main function of this prison school district is to prepare men and women in prison for obtaining a General Equivalency Diploma (GED). This is done through a reading program for those who are below the sixth grade level. In addition, thirty-seven courses are taught through Windham's Career and Technology Education program (CTE).

Certain colleges and universities offer courses to offenders in conjunction with approved degree plans within space provided by the participating prison units. A masters degree program is offered in one location, the Ramsey I Unit, through the University of Houston—Clear Lake. Offender enrollees must arrange for payment of the courses they take. However, they may be allowed to take one course per semester by signing an agreement to pay the state for the course upon their release.

Texas' prison newspaper, *The Echo*, is circulated within prisons throughout the state and is mailed to individual subscribers in the free world. Since 1928, with occasional lapses, *The Echo* has engaged its readers in matters related to life in Texas prisons. In 2001, the four inmates who prepared each issue of the paper were relieved of their duties. When control of the paper was turned over to the Windham School District, the special kind of writing that once graced the pages of *The Echo* was replaced by words held captive by administered conformity.

TRAVELING TEXAS

The movement of prisoners from one place to another is a daily occurrence and is carried out at great expense to the people of Texas. According to the Open Records Coordinator of the TDCJ, there were 4,543,888 miles of offender transportation between September 1, 2006 and August 31, 2007. Faded white buses, along with some smaller white vans, are regularly seen along the highways and narrow country roads on their way between prisons. Offenders who are to be transferred from one location to another are not told in advance. Convicts with long sentences may end up at a prison where they have served time before. Sometimes, a maintenance boss will arrange to have a particular offender transferred in order to fill a special work need. Texas prisoners who find themselves "on the road again" often think about what the food will be like in their "new place" or if they will meet up with someone they have known elsewhere. New arrivals are pleased if they encounter a "home-boy," maybe someone they can talk to about old times and things they did before they started traveling Texas in prison vans.

EXPERIENCING PRISON
AT THE WILLIAM P. HOBBY UNIT

Carolyn describes her first hours as a new arrival at the William P. Hobby Unit:

> I remember very clearly the day of my arrival at the William P. Hobby Prison Unit in Marlin, Texas, in September 1996. I arrived in a prison bus handcuffed to a stranger. I was wearing a pair of sunglasses I had purchased at the Gatesville Reception Unit where women are regularly processed in and out of prison. I remember wondering to myself if I would ever see the day when I would be one of the ones processing out, because at that moment my ten-year sentence seemed like an eternity in front of me. I hold a vivid memory of my first glimpse of the buildings as the bus pulled into the back gate area where we would be deposited. I'm not sure what I expected. It seems ridiculous to me now that I would somehow expect something different or better. In the county jail prior to my transfer to prison, the repeat offenders described prison as being like a college campus behind a fence lined with razor wire. In retrospect, I don't think any of the people making that comparison had ever even seen a college campus. The William P. Hobby Unit looked nothing like any college campus I had ever seen or been on.
>
> When I stepped off the bus a female officer took off my sunglasses before she took off my handcuffs. She tossed the sunglasses to the ground. I did not say a word but I am sure that the expression on my face betrayed me by revealing my shock and shame at the realization of where my own actions had brought me. The officer said, 'I know you bought the sunglasses at Gatesville. They allow them on other units but I guess they didn't tell you that the sun doesn't shine on Happy Hobby.' My education was underway.
>
> A new arrival of offenders is known as a 'chain.' After being relieved of sunglasses and handcuffs, the other members of the 'chain' and I were seated in a fenced waiting area outside of the command building. This particular area was known as the 'cage.' While sitting in the 'cage' waiting for a housing and job assignment, I noticed a rather thick cloud of smoke filtering out of a cell window in the building closest to the command building. Suddenly, there

was quite a commotion; numerous officers in gray uniforms were running past the 'cage' heading in the direction of the disturbance. Some of the officers were carrying video cameras and others were carrying riot garb but none of them noticed a fight between two offenders out close to the 'cage.' They were focused on where the smoke was coming from. The two offenders tired of fighting, in fact they wore themselves out. Each one was bleeding from the nose. They quickly disappeared without detection and more than likely without any resolution to their problem. The large group of officers eventually escorted two offenders in handcuffs out of the building where the smoke had been coming from. Word got back quickly to those of us who were in the 'cage' that the two offenders wanted to be moved so they set clothes and newspapers on fire in their cell. At the time I wondered how they could possibly set a fire. I soon learned about how 'illegal' cigarettes are lit using a pencil lead and an electrical outlet. (Where there is a will, there is a way and, in prison, there is certainly enough 'time' to figure out a way.)

As I and the other newcomers made our way to the buildings we were assigned, the sun disappeared for the day. On our way, we were observed and heckled by offenders shouting, among other things, 'fresh meat.' I'm sure that I looked very haggard and shell shocked by the time I arrived at my assigned cell. A very unfriendly looking woman was peering out of the wire mesh opening in the cell door. She was scowling. Not saying anything, she just stared at me with utter disdain. This was day one of my incarceration experience at the Hobby Unit. (As it turned out, the scowling woman who became my 'cellie' was not so bad after all. We got along just fine. Later, we laughed about the scowl which I soon realized was nothing more than a defense mechanism.)

When our daughter first arrived at the William P. Hobby Unit, life was hard for her and there were dangers she had not previously encountered. She went through tests from prison-hardened inmates. There were threats, offers of friendship, and pressures designed to break down her resistance. Even a shared cell, protective in certain ways, was not free from the kind of door tampering that created a potential danger. She quickly discovered that inmates can slip certain substances into the latch area of the cell door that will prevent it from locking, thereby rendering the cell occupants vulnerable to unwelcome visitors.

An incident occurred not long after Carolyn arrived at the Hobby Unit that served to place an unusual kind of safety shield around her. As she entered the shower area one morning, she was greeted by the piercing scream of a woman emerging from a shower stall. The problem, quickly perceived, was that the water was ice cold. Other women, waiting to see if the water would get warm, watched with curiosity as this "newcomer" entered the shower. They were prepared to identify her as an "easy mark" since she seemed totally oblivious to the meaning of the scream. Carolyn immediately recognized a chance to disarm those who might cause her some trouble. She did not turn around. Instead, steeling herself for the shock, she stepped into the shower and remained totally silent as the icy water hit her. She remained in the shower some time, enduring the freezing stream without making a sound. Those who were ready for a good laugh at her expense were speechless. She finally emerged from the shower just as if it had been a delightful, relaxing experience. After proving to themselves that the water had not gotten warmer, the onlookers could only whisper to each other in bewilderment.

The shower story was told around the dorm and this special inmate gained the reputation of one who was a mystery. Being perceived in this way gave her a feeling of safety. She knew that if the other inmates have someone "figured out" they will frequently impose their intimidating design upon them in order to obtain certain goods or services. Quick thinking bought her additional time as the blessing of faith assurances, gained and given, provided for her an enduring and unassailable protection.

Carolyn describes the two main types of housing at the William P. Hobby Unit:

> The first type of housing I entered at Hobby was a 'cell block' consisting of four buildings each one divided into three dorms. Each dorm has twenty-two cells upstairs and twenty-two downstairs. An individual cell is built to hold two offenders. It contains two bunks and a toilet. There is no possibility of privacy between cellmates but this type of housing provides a degree of separation from others living in the dorm. The key to life in the block is getting along with your 'cellie.' The reality, however, is that number one, we are women and, number two, we are strangers. We have an endless range of psycho-social issues and, added to that, we are criminals. Out of this equation, it should not be a surprise to anyone that seldom is a 'match' made in a closet size cell. Officers enter the dorms each hour between six in the morning and ten at night to let offenders in or out of their cells. Officers also enter the dorms at 'count time.' Since there are no surveillance cameras in

these dorms or cells, the majority of unstructured time in the cell is spent out of sight of any officer.

There are many conflicts that arise between cellies. One common dispute arises when one of them starts washing clothes in the toilet and the other one needs to use the toilet for its intended purpose. Many arguments and fights erupt because of failures in consideration and common courtesy. There are a few of us who refuse to surrender to the 'norm.' We refuse to wash clothes in a toilet.

The other type of housing on this unit is the 'open dorm,' where I was moved after over four years in a cell. It is a barn-like structure divided into four dorms lined with cubicles upstairs and downstairs. The advantage of this type of housing is that you don't have to wait to be let out of a cell each hour. There is open access to the cubicles and the day room area. The downside here is that there is absolutely no privacy because your neighbors live in extremely close proximity to you. There are twelve surveillance cameras in the dorm to monitor activity. Offenders have learned how to reduce the visual acuity of the surveillance by applying a mixture of petroleum jelly and baby powder to the bristles of a long-handled broom and touching the glass encasement of the camera lens. By the time the officer investigates the obstruction of the lens, the offenders have completed the activity that they wanted to conceal.

On-the-job training followed Carolyn's certification as a Locksmith and Door Closer Mechanic at the William P. Hobby Unit. When the offender who held the locksmith position was released, Carolyn was given the job. Here are some of the thoughts she shared with us about her prison profession.

> A physical prison is clearly defined with its high security locks and over-sized keys representing the epitome of control over entry, access, and exit. The barriers appear all-powerful; formidable and yet, in reality, with a few simple tools, prison locks are easily defeated and disassembled. The prisons of addiction, of abuse, of violent haphazard, dishonest living; these are not so easily accessed. There are no pre-fabricated keys. There are no schematics. The Texas Department of Criminal Justice taught me the mechanics of unlocking and opening the toughest of doors. My job assignment for my entire incarceration thus far has been in the maintenance department as the prison locksmith and door closer mechanic. I work hard to keep myself locked in. The position has served me well and it is rather a paradox—'the inmate prison locksmith.' At

the beginning of this journey, I could have never imagined the whole picture of what was to come.

PRISON VISITATION

There are family members who travel each week to visit a loved one in a Texas prison for the first time. Quite often they arrive without any prior knowledge of reasons why their visit could be denied. Sometimes visitors appear at the prison during the week, not realizing that visitation days are limited to Saturday and Sunday. Many visitors arrive to see a loved one only to be told that their names are not on the offender's approved list of visitors (the number of approved visitors cannot exceed ten). Others arrive and discover, to their dismay, that someone else has already visited the one they have come to see (only one visit is allowed per weekend) or that he or she has been transferred to another facility.

Visits are for two hours, between 8:00 a.m. and 5:00 p.m., except in cases where the warden may approve a four-hour visit for those who must travel over 300 miles one way. Or, these long distance visitors may be permitted to visit two hours on Saturday and two hours on Sunday. Only two adults can visit at any one time. Four children under sixteen years of age can visit if they are in the company of one or two adults who have been approved for visitation. New visitation guidelines, as of July 18, 2008, allow for certain visitation opportunities on Fridays.

The Texas offender visitation rules include a dress code that is subject to broad interpretation. Specifically, shorts and sleeveless shirts or blouses are unacceptable, as well as items of clothing that are all white (white being the color of offender clothing). Shirts with profanity or offensive language on them are not permitted. In addition, no cell phones, letters, pictures, paper money, or printed material of any kind can be brought into the building.

Visitors sometimes spend hours waiting outside, in all kinds of weather, for a place inside to become available for a visit. Those who come to visit during the holidays can generally expect a long wait. Frustration always mounts as a result of the inconsistent rulings applied by the prison's visitation staff from one weekend to another. This occurs, for example, when a certain way of dress is denied that on a previous visit was accepted without question. Marilyn and I tell visitors who have concerns about visitation rules, or any problem related to a loved one's life in the prison, to ask to see the duty officer in charge during the weekend.

Regular visits take place as visitors, seated on one side of the Plexiglas barrier, talk to offenders on the other side. In most situations, they talk by way of a telephone hook-up. Contact visits are the most desirable. They take place at tables in the visitation room where offender and visitors are seated at a table together and are allowed a hug at the beginning and at the end of the visit. Contact visit eligibility, generally allowed after an offender has been located at a facility for 90 days, is limited to the offender's closest relatives. The most serious offender disciplinary cases can result in all visitation privileges being suspended or, less seriously, in a period of time when only regular visits are permitted.

Wherever men, women, and children enter prisons to visit loved ones there is legitimate concern over how they will be treated by prison personnel. The prison emphasis on security normally requires visitors, even the children, to be scanned electronically after emptying their pockets. The officers working visitation who are courteous in carrying out this assignment prove that security need not be placed in jeopardy by good treatment. I understand, however, why opinions harden and visitation rules change when visitors direct their anger and resentment against those who work for the prison. The negative human interaction coming from prison's dark side shows a strange land where the voice of singing is too seldom lifted above the reigning sadness of each weary day.

VISITATION RELIEF

Hospitality Houses and Family Visitors' Centers in Texas are found in a few areas of the state where there is a heavy concentration of prisoners. The houses provide overnight lodging for those who travel long distances to visit with loved ones. Little or no charge is assessed by these church-supported facilities. Family Visitors' Centers offer relief to prison visitors by providing a place to rest. In all of these locations, whether they are on prison land or private land, volunteers extend gestures of hospitality, including information and refreshments, to those who come to visit loved ones. In addition, they generally have clothing items to loan to visitors who arrive not dressed according to prison guidelines.

A story appearing in Texas newspapers in May of 2007 revealed that the Texas Legislature had approved, after years of denying its passage, a bill to allow telephone calls to be made from prison by Texas inmates, perhaps beginning sometime in 2008. This was good news for relatives and friends who are never, or seldom ever, able to visit a loved one in prison.

A WATER SUPPLY PROBLEM

On an April Sunday, after arriving for our visit, Marilyn and I learned that the Hobby Unit was having a problem with their water supply. The source of the prison's liquid lifeline was the city of Marlin and the news that reached the offenders was that Marlin's filtering equipment had failed and that the entire system was shut down pending its repair.

Not only was drinking water unavailable at the Hobby Unit, but water to flush the commodes was also absent. Chaos ensued even as the prison started trucking in water for drinking purposes and portable toilets were set up to replace the normal waste disposal system. The drinking water, we were told, was laced with disinfectant chemicals and had a terrible taste. In addition, only two portable toilets were set up for use by hundreds of women, resulting in severe discomfort and long lines. Restroom facilities were working in the visitation area but water, normally available in the vending machines, was sold out. We did not have to hear all the details of how horrible life was for the women offenders. We understood how the odor drifting in and around the buildings was nauseating and how anger and frustration was at a very high level. We were told that one family, after completing their visit, drove directly to a television station in Waco where they reported the Hobby problems. That evening, the story appeared on television stations in the Waco area showing the warden as she sought to allay public concern over the problem the women prisoners were having. The following week, water for flushing was restored and a massive cleanup was started.

CALMED BY THE SINGING OF A BIRD

Two weeks later, with agitation among the visitors still running high, we waited in line outside the Hobby Unit gatehouse for our visit. Suddenly, a Texas mockingbird started singing. I imagined that it had been sent by God to soothe the anger and restlessness experienced by relatives and friends of women offenders, including children who had been brought to visit their mothers. The bird, perched almost out of sight on the slanted gatehouse roof, sang without stopping for at least ten minutes. I was surprised when the angry voices of some of those waiting in line, expressing negative comments about the prison and its employees, grew quiet. It was like a gift from heaven. The exquisitely clear tones of the mockingbird's song charmed into silence those who waited. When the bird flew away, a small boy in the line started whistling, innocently, and almost reverently, some notes of the mockingbird's song we had just heard. I thought how amazing it was that the singing of a bird was able to bring calm to those who were waiting.

GROWING OLD IN TEXAS PRISONS

Anyone serving time in a Texas prison is officially considered to be "elderly" when they reach the age of fifty-five. This particular age group of the prison population is scattered throughout the state in over one hundred locations. When old-age disabilities come to those in prison they are kept with the general population for as long as they are able to get around without assistance. The Estelle Unit near Huntsville is the only one in the system with sixty beds designated as a geriatric facility. As of October 31, 2007, this facility was home to twenty of the sixty-eight Texas prisoners who were over 80 years of age, including the oldest Texas prisoner who was eighty-nine years of age.[6] Younger offenders who are approved for this duty by the prison management provide an important level of custodial assistance for these "Estelle Elders."

In rare instances, elderly prisoners may be released toward the end of their lives to family members who are available and who will accept them. The requirements of this form of release are so strict that very few of those who are eligible for consideration ever obtain it. Many die each year while their applications are being processed.

CRISIS SITUATIONS

When a close relative of a prisoner is seriously ill, the chaplain can sometimes arrange for a telephone call to wherever the relative is located. These carefully monitored calls may include another family member who is at the bedside. When death comes to a close relative of an offender, there is a slight chance that the offender will be granted permission to attend the funeral. Only one of the many disqualifying conditions needs to exist for

6. Information supplied by Alicia Frezia-King, Open Records Act Coordinator, TDCJ Executive Services.

this privilege to be denied. When the offender's status allows attendance at a loved one's funeral, an escort is provided.

There is no sadder news coming out of the prison to family members on the outside than that their loved one in prison has died. A supportive family, receiving the shock of such news, will have questions about the conditions surrounding the death. A good prison chaplain is important in fulfilling the need to show concern for those to whom such calls are made.

When Marilyn and I worked as volunteer chaplains at the L. G. Plane State Jail for women, under the direction of Chaplain Glory Siller, I was in the position of having to call the family of an incarcerated woman who had died from a heart attack. It was a difficult responsibility, requiring that I call upon all of the faith resources for difficult times through which I have guided others during my years as a minister. In addition, I was asked by the ranking officer to go out to the dorm where the woman had been housed to talk with the offenders who lived around the deceased. I will not forget how they looked that day, gathered in an almost complete circle around me. As I spoke to those who lived under the daily load of despair and desperation, my greatest challenge was to present myself as one who cared for them. I sought, in those brief moments, to display hopefulness where hope was in short supply and to address, as simply as possible, the uncertainties and fears that a death in their midst had brought upon them. Finally, as the women in their white prison garb stood listening with sad faces, I recited the words of the twenty-third Psalm before I concluded with a prayer.

THOSE FOR WHOM NO BELL TOLLS

When a Texas prisoner dies, the normal procedure is to release the body to the designated contact person. When the contact person is not available, or no plans are on file regarding interment elsewhere, the prison system provides a place in the prison burial ground. To serve this purpose, the Captain Joe Byrd Cemetery is a well-maintained burial site overshadowed by beautiful pine trees in Huntsville, Texas.

Deceased Texas prisoners for decades had only their prison numbers to identify them on their grave markers.[7] Warden Jim Willit, who

7. On a hot July day, Marilyn and I drove up to Huntsville to see the Texas Prison Museum and to visit with the director of that facility, Jim Willit, former warden of the Huntsville Prison Unit. In talking about the prison cemetery, he told us that many years ago prisoners were buried in plots near the prison in which they died and that in several instances their names were on the markers. He went on to say that in other locations

was responsible at the time for the cemetery operation, listened to inmate family members and decided it was time to make a change. Now, and since January of 2000, men and women who die in a Texas prison, and whose remains are interred in the Captain Joe Byrd Cemetery, have their names cut into the stones that mark their graves. A warden who listened, and who cared enough to act, has given these prisoners, who for so long were only a number, a final gift of respect—their names.

For those who are interested, there is a deeply touching story of a particular prisoner's death inside a Texas prison in the Spring 2008 issue of *TIFA Contact*, a newsletter published by the Texas Inmate Families Association.[8] The man who died, and who is so respectfully remembered, was buried in the Captain Joe Byrd Cemetery on April 17, 2008.

The release to free-world soil of the bodies of those whose earthly lives end in prison does not attract widespread attention. But for family members or friends of a deceased prisoner, there is a special kind of remembering upon such an occasion. In addition, there are people who live in God's world who feel diminished by "every man's death," even those for whom no bell tolls.

DAVID RUIZ

David Ruiz, a man who spent only four years of his adult life outside of prison, is credited with changing Texas prisons by writing the lawsuit that has since been called "Ruiz v. Estelle." At first, during the early seventies, his attempts to obtain a hearing were rejected and he was repeatedly punished for persisting. Finally, U. S. District Court Judge William Wayne Justice accepted his class action lawsuit in 1974. The trial started in 1978 and concluded a year later. The sweeping changes, ordered by Judge Justice, required the expenditure of billions of dollars to relieve overcrowding in Texas prisons along with other significant reforms. David Ruiz, a convicted criminal, leaves his name on many legal documents and textbooks on crime and punishment. To those who celebrate his life for the results his work obtained for better treatment of prisoners, his name stands for courage. He died in a prison hospital in Galveston, Texas, on November 12, 2005. According to those close to Ruiz who mourned his passing, he

---

where graves have been found, there were no markers on them at all.

8. Readers may request of a copy of the article, "Death and the Texas Prison," by emailing tifa@tifa.org.

was repeatedly punished during his prison years and inexcusably denied proper medical care.

ANSWERING THE CALL

I started visiting Victor McCord at the Ellis Unit near Huntsville as the result of a call that went out from Bishop Dan Solomon, presider of the Louisiana Conference of the United Methodist Church. I learned that, as a boy, Victor was impressed by the kindness he received from the pastor of the Methodist church in Corpus Christi, Texas, that he attended with his mother. The pastor's name was Dan Solomon.

I learned a lot about prison life from Victor McCord during the years I checked in at the Ellis Unit. At the time my approved visits as a minister started, Victor was a minimum custody trusty who was allowed to drive a truck for maintenance work at prison units within a fairly wide circle around Huntsville. Our visits took place where Death Row inmates visited friends and family (weekday visits are allowed for Death Row inmates). Sometimes the noise of visitors talking all around us was a distraction. While McCord was not brought into the cubicle in handcuffs like the others, the visitation area itself was restrictive.

After a well-publicized escape attempt by several Death Row inmates on Thanksgiving Day of 1998, changes were made rather quickly. First, the warden was given another assignment. Second, a decision came down that took away the jobs done by Death Row prisoners in the prison garment factory. Finally, the world received the news that the men on Texas' Death Row were going to be moved to a newer, and supposedly more secure, prison unit across the Trinity River to the east, near the town of Livingston, Texas.

Several of the Death Row inmates had already been moved from the Ellis Unit when I visited there in February of 2000. When I came again in March, all of them were gone and everything had changed. The car I was driving was not inspected at the station along the entry road. Then, after I parked my car, I was surprised to discover that no one was in the gatehouse. An officer in the gate tower lowered a bucket on a rope and asked me to drop my driver's license into it. After pulling it up, she called inside to make sure I was approved to visit. I was surprised that I was not asked to empty my pockets and that I was not scanned electronically.

Inside the building, I stopped to obtain the number of the location where I would be seated for my visit and, surprisingly, was told I didn't need one. I turned the corner near the location where before I had always heard the sound of many voices. Silence reigned. The passageway behind the visitation cubicles, where the prisoners and their escorts usually came and went at visitation time, was empty. Victor was waiting in an open section, not inside a cubicle. The only other person in sight was a correctional officer seated not far away. Death Row was gone.

The two of us talked easily together and when we received the signal that our visit was over, our hands touched the glass, with palms facing each other, as I prayed. In the sanctuary of our private space, quiet as never before, I did not have to pray over the noise of many voices. I thought how regular visitors and friends might experience particular feelings of loss and uncertainty, along with the Death Row inmates, over the move to another facility. And yet, I knew that God would not be without witnesses wherever death seeks to have the last word.

In August of 2001, my minister visits to the Ellis Unit came to an end. Marilyn and I were glad that Victor's long stay in prison was over even though he would be on parole for many years following his release. An aftercare facility accepted him upon our recommendation and a United Methodist congregation not far away welcomed him into their fellowship. After spending several months as a resident of Wholeway House, he obtained a good job which became, as he told me later, his life. From time to time, he asked me: "What can I do to repay you for what you have done for me?" My answer remained the same: "By never going back to prison."

When Death Row was moved to the Terrell Unit in Livingston, Charles Terrell, former Chairman of the Texas Board of Criminal Justice, requested that his name no longer be used to identify the prison. Some people understood that he didn't want his name on a prison that housed those who were awaiting execution by the state. Alan B. Polunsky, who had just completed his tenure as chairman of the board, accepted that dubious honor.

DEATH ROW RE-VISITED

The pastor of a United Methodist church in a little town in Central Texas, mid-way between Houston and San Antonio, called to ask if I would talk with a woman in her church whose grandson was being held in the Harris

County Jail on a murder charge. I agreed to do so and later, in the course of my telephone conversation with her, while listening to her words of faith, hope, and love, was convinced that I should visit her grandson (whose name I am withholding out of respect to all parties). I was able to visit him several times at the jail prior to his trial, placing no judgment of guilt or innocence upon him. I met his grandmother toward the end of his trial and felt a deep sadness for her over what seemed certain to be bad news.

When I heard of the jury's guilty verdict and the sentence of death that accompanied it, I thought at once of how this caring grandmother would feel when she heard the news. I was convinced that I could not write "finished" to my involvement. As soon as I learned of her grandson's transfer from the Harris County Jail to the Polunsky Unit, I submitted my ministerial credentials to the warden's office there and was approved to visit him.

Maundy Thursday of Holy Week marked the date when I made my first trip to the Livingston location of Texas' Death Row. The first section of any travel length from our home east of Houston was U.S. Highway 90, and this took me all the way to the town of Liberty. From there, I went north on State Highway 146 to Livingston. Along that stretch of highway, I saw houses surrounded by beautiful red azaleas and, where the highway bordered the Big Thicket National Preserve, white dogwood blossoms, visible against the forest greenery. These natural wonders helped to ease my anxious thoughts concerning the prison appointment I was about to keep.

When I reached Livingston, I turned west on U.S. Highway 190. After passing the Polk County Court House on the town square and, at length, going under U. S. Highway 59 as it cuts through the fringe of this East Texas town, a marker told me to turn left on Farm Road 350 South. A winding country road soon brought me into sight of the Alan B. Polunsky Unit.

The first building I entered was an unusually spacious gatehouse where an officer, using the familiar electronic wand, checked me carefully. Although I had completely emptied my pockets, the wand kept issuing a warning buzz. I removed the cross that hung around my neck, then my belt and, finally, my shoes. At last, seeming to tire of the effort, the officer shrugged and waved me toward the door. After passing through a controlled door and gate, I followed a long sidewalk, bordered on each side with blooming flowers, which led to the main building. Once inside, I went through two more carefully monitored doors into the visitation area. There, the officer on duty gave me a numbered location where I was asked to wait.

Two correctional officers escorted the tall young man, who I immediately recognized from my visits with him in Houston, into a cubicle facing where I waited on the other side of the glass. He stepped inside and stuck his handcuffed hands back through a small opening in the door and, while leaning forward, waited until his hands were freed. After visiting over our phone connection about family members and prison conditions, I opened my pocket size copy of the New Testament and Psalms. The lesson I read from Matthew's gospel focused on Jesus and his disciples at the Upper Room meal in Jerusalem prior to his capture, trial, and crucifixion. I told him that Christians, in remembrance of Jesus, would be taking part in The Lord's Supper services that evening. I repeated to him the words we use in offering members of the family of faith the gifts of bread and wine that link us to that special meal. I sought to explain what makes this service so special to those who celebrate their fellowship in Christ. Finally, when I was told that we had five more minutes, I offered a prayer for him. He thanked me for coming and asked if I would call his grandmother.

Over the years when I have visited on the Polunsky Unit, I have been able to greet one or more of the faithful who regularly share the love of Jesus with prisoners. These faithful ones are both clergypersons and laypersons who spend time on Death Row offering a message of redemption to those who dwell in the darkest corner of the prison system. I am especially impressed with Catherine Cox, a gracious lady in her eighties, who represents the Salvation Army. She drives from Dallas once a week to visit a number of men on Death Row. We speak briefly, when the time of our visitation coincides, in acknowledgment of our common objective.

On one of my visits, after learning that the grandmother and grandfather of the man I visit had kept him during the first year of his life, he told me that his great-grandfather was a violin craftsman who came to this country from Germany. This, I imagined, could help to account for his love of classical music, especially the works of German composers. On another occasion, I was surprised to learn that his prison reading had taken him into the world of Christian martyrdom. He brought up the name of Bishop Polycarp of Smyrna. His interest brought to my mind a stirring reference to Bishop Polycarp made by Dr. W. Richey Hogg who taught Church History at Perkins School of Theology many years ago. I remembered how he closed the lesson by telling us how Polycarp, when given one last chance to renounce the faith, replied: "For eighty-six years I have served my Master. He has never let me down. Why should I deny him now?" Later, I wondered why anyone facing such a different kind of death sentence would bring up the subject. Was it his way of becoming more visible to me or was it a hint that he was thinking about one last chance to accept the faith? I have concluded that in addition to his need to identify himself to me, he was curious about the kind of faith I represented. Hope exists for both of us that something will happen to preserve his life.

I regularly talked by telephone with the lady who was so grateful for my visits with her grandson and Marilyn and I received many cards of thanks from her. One day she mentioned her desire to visit her grandson at the Polunsky Unit, no matter how tragic the circumstances. As it turned out, she has never been able to do so since the promises made by others to take her were never fulfilled. Actually, I think they felt as if it would be too much for her.

> In the town of Huntsville, Texas, during the late afternoon of each day when an execution is scheduled, people enter St. Stephen's Episcopal Church to participate in 'A Liturgy on the Day of an Execution.' Prayer is offered for everyone involved in what will take place just off the town square. The people of God, as a part of their calling of faith, respond from the depths of their hearts.[9]

9. *Living Next Door to the Death House,* a book written by Virginia Stem Owens and David Clinton Owens, concludes with the complete service after offering an absorbing story of Huntsville, Texas, and the affect death penalty executions have upon many of its citizens.

6

Complaint and Compliance

The words of the mouth are deep waters;
the fountain of wisdom is a gushing stream.

—Proverbs 18:4

COMPLAINTS ARE HEARD IN prisons across the land and the prison requirements of compliance are repeatedly emphasized. In a broad sense, prison inmates spend their days somewhere along a line between resistance (complaint) and acceptance (compliance), between protesting real or imaginary wrongs on one hand and keeping cool on the other. Complaints are tied to unpleasant disruptions of the daily routine and to personally disturbing treatment by prison personnel. A few of those in prison are able to maintain a delicate balance between breathing threats against the absurdities and finding moments of silence apart from the constraints they represent. Compliance, on the other hand, is a dependable way of living in prison that accepts the hardships while praying for a purposeful future. Outside of either category, there are those in prison whose actions can only identify them as rebels. They display a volatile mix of anger, abrasiveness, and thirst for control while responding to each deprivation or disciplinary action not as something to complain about or comply with but as acts of disrespect requiring some form of retaliation.

COMPLAINT

With my voice I cry to the Lord;
with my voice I make supplication to the Lord.
I pour out my complaint before him;
I tell my trouble before him.

—Psalm 142:1–2

Prison life holds a minefield of complaint triggers and each new day brings many of the same complaints as the day before. Prison inmates complain about the harshness with which the prison staff exercises control over them. They complain about prison food and prison living conditions. In addition, there are complaints about how family members have abandoned them. The weaker inmates, who suffer threats and violent treatment at the hands of predatory inmates, complain in silent bitterness over what they are forced to endure.

Prison complaints can be personal or they can be about the broader problems that affect everyone in prison. They can range from the most frivolous to the most serious, from the normal discomforts of prison living to the utter despair of survival under conditions unfit for human habitation. They can be bold assertions of fact or boring recitals of imagined entitlements.

Men and women in prison who have come to terms with their misdeeds appreciate anyone from the outside who cares enough to listen to the stories of what they face from day to day. When they are granted the privilege of opening up to someone who is concerned about them, someone they respect, the possibilities of exaggeration and deceit are minimized. Also, when prisoners reach a certain level of desperation that causes them to raise their voices in complaint to God, they avoid the critical judgment leveled against those who characteristically do nothing but complain.

Complaints arising from circumstances apart from the common deprivations of prison life should be filed through prison channels as grievances, even at the risk of reprisals, as a warning to the prison and as an effort to obtain some reasonable form of satisfaction. Conditions that warrant such action include corporal punishment, verbal harassment, deprivation of necessary health care, failure to provide adequate nutrition, and limitation of the right to send and receive mail. Being quiet too long limits the possibility of obtaining a satisfactory resolution of such problems. The one who does nothing could be compared to the psalmist who said:

> *I was silent and still;*
> *I held my peace to no avail;*
> *my distress grew worse,*

—Psalm 39:2

Family members who realize what prison is doing to their loved ones are subject to feelings of helplessness and despair. Some cry out to God in the manner and spirit of the psalmists. Others, while asking for God's help, speak directly to the prison management about specific problems. One day, while I was greeting prison visitors, I met a woman (whom I will call Mrs. Walker) who had come to visit her son at the L. V. Hightower Unit. After learning my name and what I was doing, she became comfortable enough to tell me about her son being attacked at another Texas prison and having two of his teeth knocked out.

As Mrs. Walker's story unfolded, I heard her say how, at first, she assumed the prison dentist would correct the damage to her son's teeth. When nothing happened, she decided to speak to the warden of the prison. At first, he shrugged off her complaint, saying that he did not have responsibility over dental services. Mrs. Walker did not go home and quietly grieve over the insensitivity to her son's needs. She decided that threatened publicity might get some action but she very wisely went to the warden first and made her case known to him. Obviously affected by the righteous anger and indignation she expressed, the warden reconsidered his position. I can still remember how she described the warden's response, beginning with the words, "Now, Mrs. Walker . . . " Not long afterward, she was pleased to say, her son received the prison equivalent of an appointment to see the dentist and the corrective work was started.

The stories told about what takes place in prisons sometimes enlarge upon the truth or leave out some of the facts. As a result, I am cautious about repeating stories of prison incidents that I am told by offenders or their family members and friends. In the case of Mrs. Walker's story, however, I have no such hesitancy. The look in her eyes and the forcefulness of her words made me a believer.

COMPLIANCE

Trust in the Lord, and do good;
so you will live in the land and enjoy security.
Take delight in the Lord,
and he will give you the desires of your heart.

—Psalm 37:34

The compliance theme, as reflected by the psalmist, is hard for many of those who are new to prison life to accept. These offenders soon learn, however, that compliance is a major theme of prison management. The prison itself is held to compliance operational guidelines and each prison inmate hears the compliance tune played over and over in ways that focus upon how they live and what they are supposed to do throughout each day.

A compliant attitude in prison often helps to promote healing and a readiness for release. This means accepting regulations and work requests out of an inner resolve to deal as honestly with the prison system as possible. Those who follow this path reject routine complaining and do not allow the treatment they receive from other offenders or the demeaning treatment of prison employees to control their thoughts and actions. Songs of overcoming anger, doubt, and fear can strengthen the confidence needed to walk the tight line of security demands and offender provocation. The best kind of compliance isn't about obtaining quick or easy answers nor is it a compromise for the sake of momentary gain. It is about a manner of living that is trustworthy in an environment where suspicion and distrust are common.

Compliance is involved in the secret of how beautiful flowers can bloom in the unpromising soil of a prison garden. This thought comes from a true story told in a devotional guide for prisoners called *Prisoner to Prisoner*, published by Kairos Prison Ministry of Ohio and the Marion Correctional Institution. I can easily imagine that if a certain offender there had not been compliant in the best way, he might never have succeeded in getting permission to create an English-style garden inside the walls, transforming the very soul of the prison in the process. With the help of prison companions, this particular individual made a difference, not only in the lives of offenders but also in the lives of correctional personnel and those who came to visit loved ones. The Marion Correctional

Institution became something more than just a place of anger, sadness, and desolation through the persistence of one particular inmate who possessed a talent for growing plants and flowers. We should remember how seeds of good intent can spring to life in the most unlikely place, a prison, thereby dispelling the pessimistic conclusions about how nothing good can happen where human life is so terribly devalued.

The watchful fear generated by knowing how things are in prison comes more readily to older prisoners who have learned how to make realistic assessments of potential danger. Tossed about in the roiling current of prison life, the "old cons," having grown wiser by learning when to be afraid, have been known to lose their rebellious nature and earlier propensity to cause trouble. When they have been claimed, body and soul, by the prison, and without anything left to prove, they settle into the desultory routine of "old convicts," having much in common with "old guards" with whom they share "old stories" of life in prison.

Compliance of another kind is noticed in the lives of those who actually become content with the kind of life prison offers them. These individuals, both men and women, accept prison over the trouble and strife they were never able to escape in the outside world. Carolyn writes about her experience of this kind of compliance.

> When I was in the county jail, I met a young woman who was a prostitute and a heroin addict. She described her way of life to me as one that included regular trips to jail to clean up, to get medical attention, to get good sleep, and to eat and gain weight. All of this would prepare her for another stint on the street. Another example comes from the Hobby Unit. A woman who had five children described her life at home as being one constant struggle with never enough money to make ends meet. She was a trusty who worked mowing grass and preparing the fields surrounding the prison unit for planting. She said to me: 'This is my fifth trip down. It's a vacation for me. When I'm out on my tractor in the wide open field watching the sun rise, hey, I'm in paradise.' To some, prison life may actually be preferable to life on the outside because basic needs are met and a circle of friends is established. When offenders return to society and are in the situation of being unemployed and broke, they may prefer to return to prison and many do whatever it takes to return.

A servile form of compliance is seen within the dark corridors of prisons where frightened inmates are subjected to threats that involve protection hustles. Their weakness diminishes whatever positive hopes for the future they might at one time have entertained. For those in prison who live in constant dread and fear, God's people respond with the prayerful entreaty, "Lord, have mercy!"

Family members who lean toward being cautiously compliant do not seek out the warden unless there is a clear and continuous danger to the safety, health, or well-being of their loved one or unless a situation arises that poses a serious problem for all of the offenders. They deal with questionable incidents by seeking answers even while understanding that many things that happen in prison are simply "the way they are." Still, family members do not rest well when they realize the dangers to which their loved ones are exposed.

SUMMARY

Complaint and compliance both hold positive and negative aspects. More than likely, the tendency we have for one or the other was formed in our earliest years and is the result of how we were brought up and the conditions through which we have lived.

Prisoners who are deeply alienated are not naturally compliant. Compliance, in their way of thinking, represents compromise and indoctrination, both considered weaknesses. Even as compliance is forced upon them, it often comes at the price of established penalties. The resistance of severely alienated offenders to any form of behavior modification is symptomatic of a rebellious attitude that views everyone who works for the prison as their enemy. On the other hand, those in prison who have the support of family members, and who take advantage of every opportunity to prepare for release, are more likely to exhibit compliance as a way of meeting the challenges that face them each day.

Family members who regularly deal with the prison system realize how complaint and compliance are both part of the prison experience. Some family members react with angry complaints when they hear about prison conditions that hurt their loved ones. Others, more conditioned to compliance, keep a watchful silence unless there is indisputable evidence that their loved ones have suffered serious injury or mistreatment. While critical situations call for reporting the problem to someone who has the authority to order an investigation, it should never be assumed that political influence can correct all the wrongs inflicted upon a subject population. Christians are able to approach prison authorities from a position of unquestionable strength only when they are armed with prayer.

While I was moving back and forth between complaint and compliance, I identified with the poetic reflections of the seventeenth-century English poet George Herbert, who wrote:

> Ah my dear angry Lord,
> Since thou dost love, yet strike;
> Cast down, yet help afford;
> Sure I will do the like.
> I will complain, yet praise;
> I will bewail, approve;
> And all my sour-sweet days
> I will lament and love.[1]

Marilyn and I never complained to the wardens of the prison although we made it a point to meet with each one and ask questions. The complaints that welled up within us from time to time were more like cries of distress over the conditions of prison life that we felt with such intensity because of the love we had for our daughter. Even through difficult times, we received answers to prayer that related specifically to the faithfulness and fortitude with which Carolyn met the greatest challenge of her life.

God regularly hears complaints about undeserved suffering. The Psalms, as an important part of our faith heritage, contain bitter complaints against God. One of the psalmists opened an insistent plea to God with the words, "Out of the depths I cried to you, O Lord. Lord, hear my voice!" (Ps 130:1–2a).

When prisoners and their family members live from day to day in compliance with prison rules and regulations, it doesn't mean they never hurt enough to voice complaints. In fact, their basic posture of compliance, in harmony with the objective of being at peace with themselves, gives their complaints a faith-directed legitimacy. When all is said and done on behalf of a loved one in prison, the answers of faith to the questions of hope for the future are offered by a benevolent God who loves us through all the changing scenes of life. The blessing of God's peace, received within and beyond the darkness of despair over what prison does to everyone,

1. Herbert, "Bitter-Sweet," 65.

finds an appropriate prayer response in the words of John Newton's lesser known hymn, "Safely Through Another Week."

> *May thy Gospel's joyful sound conquer sinners, comfort saints;*
> *Make the fruits of grace abound, bring relief for all complaints;*
> *Thus may all our sabbaths prove, till we join that church above;*
> *Thus may all our sabbaths prove, till we join that church above.*

—fourth stanza

7

Faith Practices in Prison

The exiles are called to sing songs in a strange land;
they discover in their singing that the land is not so strange.
Even this alien land is claimed for the rule of Yahweh.[1]

—Walter Brueggemann

ISRAEL'S DISPLACED PEOPLE FACED a challenge related to the practices of their faith. Their exile created a spiritual void without a temple in which to worship. The psalmist expressed his shock with the words, "O God, you have rejected us, broken our defenses; you have been angry; now restore us!" (Ps 60:1). The effective restoration of God's people began as they came together in the house of the exiled priest, Ezekiel, a practice that may have been the model for what would later be called synagogues.

Prisoners are given opportunities to worship God, to receive the counsel of a chaplain, to read the texts, and sing the songs of their faith. Some skeptics of faith practices in prison suggest that they tend to have a palliative affect upon the prison population and, as a result, management receives the greatest benefit toward its intent of control. There are supporters of such practices who promote the need to witness to lost souls as the most important reason for going into the prisons.

I have heard offenders express the opinion that worship services in prison are meaningless. One man suggested that some inmates attend services only to take advantage of the opportunity to interact with friends. While some of the services may not offer what many of those in prison need, there is some value in faithfulness and, for those who respond in a positive manner, the possibility of inmates sharing faith perspectives

1. Brueggemann, *Cadences of Home*, 129.

with each other as a result must not be dismissed. There are times during prison worship, for sure, that hope prevails over the power of the prison to inflict inner pain. Even those who have never known the blessing of peace may have their hearts opened a little at a time to the peace of Christ.

Wardens, worried about a security breach, have been known to close the prison to ministry groups. At other times church volunteers who come to conduct worship or Bible study classes are turned away at the front gate with a "schedule conflict" cited as the reason. On the other hand, faith groups are guilty, at one time or another, of not respecting the legitimate burden of control that rests upon prison employees.

CHAPLAINS

Chaplains in great numbers became part of prison systems when reform was the primary objective. As prison purposes changed, it was harder for the chaplains to "walk the line" between what prison officials expected of them and the calling of their faith. Chaplains, as representatives of a punitive system, often become occupied with duties that contribute very little to the healing of broken lives. Only those who minister to prisoners in the light of God's call to freedom are able to overcome the restrictions associated with a prisoner's loss of freedom.

Chaplains who go beyond the routine duties of filing reports and scheduling religious services are occasionally known to suffer burnout or become severely compromised in fulfilling their call to minister to prisoners. On the other hand, a dedicated chaplain's acceptance helps to heal the hurts of loneliness, anger, and false pride encountered on a daily basis in prison. Those who are faithful to their ministry find ways to introduce songs of love and mercy to the men and women they serve in prisons throughout the land.

Until I read a list of guidelines prepared by Chaplain Vance Drum of the Eastham Unit near Lovelady, Texas, entitled "Professional Correctional Chaplains," I did not realize how the chaplain's job might be complicated by having to help fulfill the requirements of the facility mandated by the U.S. Constitution. Chaplain Drum described them as "keeping the institution out of court and the warden out of prison."

When I sought to obtain approval as a minister to visit an offender at the Ramsey I Unit in Brazoria County, I immediately ran into trouble. Previously, at three other prisons, I had been given permission for my visits through the warden's office. When I called about such a visit at Ramsey, I was transferred to the chaplain and realized at once that he was going to make things difficult for me. He said he would talk to the warden concerning my request and then failed to call me back. When I tried to contact him again, he was not available. I wrote to the offender, whose name was David Hanna, and told him about the trouble I was having. He replied with a letter that revealed his thoughts about chaplains.

> I haven't had any positive experiences with TDCJ chaplains. I was put into the hospital emergency room several years ago after being assaulted by a gang when I first arrived at an Institutional Division Unit. I had a concussion; a cracked orbital around one eye; a blood clot in my other eyeball (temporarily blinding me in that eye); a broken nose; two broken ribs; and I was covered head to toe in steel-toed boot prints. When I regained consciousness the unit chaplain was at my bedside and proceeded to tell me how this beating was really my own fault and that I deserved what I got because 'I wasn't walking in the way of the Lord!' I couldn't believe he was talking to me like that.
>
> My only other experience with a unit chaplain was when I was on the Smith Unit in Lamesa, Texas. My father died and the chaplain lied to me about the requirement to attend the funeral so he wouldn't have to go through the paperwork process. By the time I found out, the funeral was over. He had done the same thing with others there. So, my experience with prison chaplains hasn't been very good. Hopefully, this one is different.

I finally, after much frustration, received a day and a time to visit David on the Ramsey I Unit. The fact that it is one of the oldest prisons in Texas heightened my interest in making the drive over to Brazoria County.

As I approached the prison, located on a vast stretch of prison farm acreage, the old red brick building fascinated me. It was clearly far removed from contemporary prison design. My visit, as it turned out, was much different from any of my previous prison visits. An employee of the prison came out to the gatehouse to meet me. The chaplain was off that day and I explained to her that I had arranged my visit through him. After going inside with the employee, I was escorted into a makeshift space where attorneys and approved ministers are allowed to conduct their visits. While waiting on a tall stool in front of a barrier made of heavy metal mesh that separates visitor and offender, I realized that I would actually be looking down upon the man I had come to visit. I waited in that unusual setting for almost an hour before going out and asking the employee who had escorted me inside if the offender I expected to see had been given a "lay-in." She admitted that this procedure, whereby he would have remained in the dorm to await his visit rather than being sent out to his work assignment, had not been followed. She assured me that they were now bringing him in from his work. I learned later that he was kept locked in the small visitation enclosure for a long time following our visit.

Since David was housed at the Ramsey I Trusty Camp, a separate and newer building within the Ramsey 1 Unit Complex, I decided to have him put my name on his approved list of visitors so that I could visit on weekends without going through the chaplain. As a result, I visited as a friend, seated comfortably at a table across from him with no barrier between us. I could have continued the tedious way of scheduling weekday visits in the old building, but such a system would have seriously compromised the opportunity for us to be equal conversation partners and, in addition, would have made his "trusty" status seem abnormally restrictive.[2]

Chaplain Richard Lopez serves the Texas Department of Criminal Justice as Director of Chaplaincy Support Services. One of his duties is assisting Death Row inmates on the day of their execution. He also speaks to family members who come to Huntsville to witness the death of their loved one. It was on just such a day that he granted me the opportunity to speak to a family facing this ordeal. My objective was to fulfill a request I received from a Holly Hall resident who knew some of the family and was aware that I would be passing through Huntsville that day on my monthly trip to the Ellis Unit. The affirmative response of Chaplain Lopez gave me an immediate cause to be thankful for his representation of the love of God in places of pain and anguish.

---

2. Trusty status affords the lowest level of restrictions that, in turn, allow those so designated to work outside without regular supervision and to receive the highest level of inmate privileges.

PRAYING AND SINGING IN PRISON

About midnight Paul and Silas were praying and singing hymns to God,
And the (other) prisoners were listening to them.

—Acts 16:25

Paul and Silas were imprisoned in Philippi for violating the customs of the city. While praying and singing, they felt the earth shake and saw the prison doors fly open. The fearful warden asked, "What shall I do to be saved?" Paul advised him to "believe in the Lord Jesus." As they came together in faithfulness, both jailer and prisoner experienced a spiritual blessing.

When it is midnight in the loneliness of prison time, praying and singing can give birth to a positive "break-out" mentality that helps to conquer fear. In addition, the spiritual gifts of praying and singing are able to move prisoners out of the self-centered claims of rights and privileges stemming from their prison-driven punishment and into opportunities that allow them to come to terms with their guilt-driven punishment.

Prayer in prison may not be too different from prayer anywhere else. When prisoners come together to pray with a chaplain or with a volunteer prayer leader, they pray for loved ones, for better treatment, for guidance in doing the right thing and, at times, for those who watch over them. When prayer does not come out of an experience of faithful living, it can easily become nothing more than a wish list addressed to an imaginary Santa Claus figure who first determines whether the subject has been good enough to merit his favors.

Prayer comes from troubled hearts by way of "sighs too deep for words." (Romans 8:26) In some instances, there are eloquently prayerful expressions that give glory to the One from whom all blessings flow. When any deeply felt sense of joy or sorrow is addressed to the God of love, it tends, even among the weakest of those "in chains," to resonate with power. Meanwhile, prayers to God on behalf of those in prison often express a longing for empty lives to be filled with the humility that empowers and to be emptied of the violence that only weakens.

When all other words fail, The Lord's Prayer, beginning with the words "Our Father, who art in heaven . . . ," never fails. However, those who pray this prayer should realize how it is not related to what we want as individuals but what God expects of those who would be his people.

The word "I" is not a part of The Lord's Prayer. The prayer Jesus taught his disciples takes individuals who imagine they are alone against the world out of themselves and names them as part of a following whose leader, a prisoner like themselves, chose peace and not war as a way to overcome the world.

There are worship services in jails and prisons that provide what many of the participants need in order to bring some semblance of order to their lives. A letter we received from Carolyn at the Galveston County Jail described such a worship service.

> We had another church service the other night. As usual, all of the inmates cling together and hold their hands high up in the air as they sing and seek freedom through prayer as the chaplain preaches on the wages of sin. During that hour, kind words are passed from inmate to inmate, words of support and encouragement, and the common use of profanity is temporarily suspended.

The conversations inmates have with each other before and after attending a worship service contain words they learned before they ever committed a crime. Sadly, for many of them, the speech models of their earlier years were those whose inflammatory language influenced the direction of their lives toward criminal behavior. Many of those in prison are serving long sentences because ungodly words opened the door of their lives to unlawful deeds. Their words continue to illustrate the tragedy that haunts their lives. Nevertheless, during the time allotted for worship, singing tends to refocus their thinking. It results, at least momentarily, in signs of caring for each other.

The most meaningful songs prisoners sing help to drain off all pretentiousness. When they are delivered to God in the spirit of the psalmist's lament or, nearer to our time, of the *blues* tradition, they bring mournful cries from the lips of those who feel convicted of their wrong-doing. Whereas the more upbeat songs contribute to *forgetting*, the slower, deeply sorrowful ones contribute to *remembering*. The songs prisoners sing provide evidence of the triumph of righteousness only when, in the constraints of their captivity, they are free enough to acknowledge their transgressions and to present themselves exactly as they are to God.

PREACHING AND STUDYING IN PRISON

Preaching about God's love entering human hearts is good news. Men and women, inside and outside of prison, respond joyfully to the "old, old story of Jesus and his love"[3] when they feel themselves addressed personally. Karl Barth, renowned Swiss theologian, preached to the prisoners of the Basel Prison in just such a manner. Along with an unpublicized ministry of prison visitation, Barth's preaching spoke directly to the prisoners' situation. In his sermon, "Blessed be the Lord," he speaks of how the Lord is ready and able to bear them up no matter what their limitations might be.

> 'He who bears us up is the God of our salvation.' This further implies that he not only bears with us, but that he also carries us *out* of the morass of our foolish and mischievous thoughts and deeds, out of our several afflictions, great and small. He carries us *through* the home-grown jungle of our imaginations and aberrations. He carries us *away* from the kingdom of death into life eternal. We cannot pull ourselves up by our own bootstraps. How could we? But he bears us up.[4]

The bread of life, offered to those behind bars, is best administered in small, easily digestible bites and with a gentleness of heart and mind. Men and women whose lives are narrowly defined by excuses or regrets often respond to sermons that are open and inviting. They listen attentively to stories that interpret the biblical text and that summon them to be alert in waiting for God. The appeal of such preaching is that it headlines the good news that God's kingdom of love and mercy has come.

Chaplain Vance Drum kindly responded to my question to him about prison preaching.

> Preaching in prison is primarily pastoral care. As the Word of God is ministered in preaching, the inmate congregation, which has generally experienced much neglect, rebellion and rejection in life, is helped to see that even though they have failed in some of the worst possible ways, there is hope and help for their life. In prison, which can be a physically and spiritually dark and dreary place, inmates need a reason to live, a purpose for their life. Preaching, and teaching, helps interpret what is happening in the inmate's life. It gives meaning, hope and inspiration—all of which are invaluable, especially in prison. I preach about once every six weeks

3. From the hymn, "I Love to Tell the Story," written by Katherine Hankey.

4. Barth, *Deliverance to the Captives*, 157–58.

in the prison. I have a great variety of ministers come to preach who represent different races and denominations. I encourage the inmates to 'eat the fish and spit out the bones,' which means to receive what meets their understanding of the Bible, and not to get too upset if they hear something with which they disagree. Ministry in prison is public ministry as opposed to denominational ministry.

I do not try to regulate too much what is preached, since we are an inter-denominational congregation in the prison. I encourage preachers to preach what they believe, but not to preach on the same subject every time they come, especially if it is a denominational 'hobby horse.' I also instruct them not to disparage other preachers or denominational groups, since that is against our policy. Good prison preachers are instructive, encouraging and hopeful. They have a balance in their teaching between law and grace. They delineate between right and wrong, between God's ways and the ways of the underworld.[5]

Chaplain Drum included this statement in his correspondence:

Valuable as preaching is, I see it mostly as an inspirational warm-up to smaller, interactive group work in Bible study, course work (such as *Experiencing God, The Purpose Driven Life*, etc.), and inter-personal relationship counseling groups. In these smaller groups there is opportunity to interact, verbalizing feelings, thoughts and conflicts, all of which is healing and healthy for people who have not been listened to very much in their lives.

Prisoners who use the Bible as nothing more than a "holy hustle" have been known to memorize long passages in order to be viewed as "immersed in the word" by church people and thereby secure a favored position with them. Sometimes the condition of broken lives brings out foolish actions through which the sacred texts are subjected to profane use. An example of this comes from a letter we received from Carolyn at the Galveston County Jail.

After church one woman describes to another a time when she was in a motel getting high with her friends. They ran out of rolling papers and were desperately searching around the room for something to use as papers. During the search, according to the

5. I received this information by email on December 7, 2005 from Rev. Vance Drum, D. Min., Chaplain of the Eastham Unit, TDCJ, and former President of the American Protestant Correctional Chaplains Association.

woman, she found the Gideon Bible in a drawer. She started tear-
ing out the pages to use instead of rolling papers. She remembers
exclaiming that they would be getting 'high and holy.' Clara is 29
years old and she claims this will be her last trip 'down.' She says
she has found Jesus. Everyone says that. I probably sound cynical
but one woman summed it up fairly honestly. She said, 'I find God
every time I come to jail and I've been coming to jail for twenty
years now.' Stripped of their drugs, now they cling to their Bibles.
That would be great if I believed that 'God' meant something more
than a 'safety net' to them. I want to acknowledge in a positive way
their professions of faith but I also crave sincerity. I seek sincerity
and peace. I seek the constancy of peace.

SEEKING PEACE

Depart from evil and do good; seek peace and pursue it.

—Psalm 35:14

A sad fact of life is that many in prison have never known peace. Some suffer from behavioral disturbances and the influences of mistreatment and
neglect that have left scars upon their minds and spirits. Their experiences
of family arguments and bitter relational conflicts have made survival the
major emphasis of their lives. Others have illnesses that need the kind of
treatment that the prison health care system does not provide.

In an environment characterized by noise and violence, peaceful
interactions are rare occurrences. Carolyn, writing from the Hobby Unit,
described such an interaction to us.

> The 'hairstylist' who left today said her goodbyes yesterday evening.
> She is one who always noticed me reading the *Upper Room* devo-
> tional each day. As she came by my cubicle, she said, 'Hey, Carolyn,
> you take care and God bless—you stay in that Upper Room, you
> hear! That Upper Room is doing the job—there's something to that
> Upper Room, I can tell.' Her comments moved me.

About mid-way through Carolyn's years of incarceration at the
William P. Hobby Unit, she started attending the Catholic services. After
a special Christmas service, she spoke of how she liked the scent of the
candles and the quiet holiness of worship that included the familiar words
of the Apostle's Creed. In addition, she regularly attended a Bible study

class taught by the Catholic deacon. This change helped to secure for her the blessing of a peace important to living without fear in a strange land.

PRISON MINISTRIES

I am the Lord, I have called you in righteousness . . . to bring out the prisoners from the dungeon, from the prison those who sit in darkness.

—Isaiah 42:6a, 42:7b

Prison ministry requires a prayerful commitment by men and women who live the faith they profess. The difficulty for many church members lies in the challenge of how to get started and how to apply one's particular gifts to such a multi-faceted endeavor. Because of the burden of crime in our cities and the way lives are violated by criminal acts, there are fears and uncertainties attached to the thought of ministering to those who have broken the law, some in such a violent manner. The nature of their separation from the freedoms the rest of us enjoy leads prisoners to be thought of as "unclean" and prisons as much like the leper colonies of earlier days. Those who make a difference in prisoners' lives embrace them in the way St. Francis of Assisi[6] did when he dismounted from his horse on the Umbrian plane and embraced the leper.

People of faith are needed who will go into the prisons as emissaries of hope in Christ. It is important to realize, however, that there are men and women in prison whose deviant behavior can confuse inexperienced volunteers. Therefore, the volunteer/offender relationship should be measured carefully. Boundaries should be established and advice should be sought from those who have ministered to prisoners for a long time. Actually, anyone who secures the right to visit a prisoner should be aware of who they are visiting and what they hope to accomplish.

Jesus, as one who suffered punishment and death at the hands of a worldly authority, has become a friend to many of those who mourn in

6. St. Francis, inspired by the love of Christ as a young man, formed a group of "brothers" who committed themselves to poverty and healing the sick. In the year 1210, he obtained the tentative approval of Pope Innocent III to permit him and his companions to be duly constituted as an order of mendicant preachers. This group later became the Franciscans. St. Francis possessed the soul of a poet, improvising hymns that brothers of the order had written. He loved the outdoors and "all creatures great and small." Marked by illnesses throughout his life, his love for the poor and sick led him to care for those who carried the dread disease of leprosy.

the lonely exile of prison. Many of the well meaning folks who decide to take Jesus into the prison are surprised to discover that he is already there. On the other hand, as one who was despised and rejected by those who were suspicious of his motives, Jesus is largely unrecognizable except to those who by grace have their eyes opened to his love and mercy.

Volunteers who visit offenders and participate in various prison ministry programs have a challenging task. In the strength of Christ, they hold up a way of thinking and acting that promotes change. Rejecting the idea of "locking them up and throwing away the key," these volunteers support the faith purpose of "looking them up and offering them the key," the key to inner peace. God's call for volunteers includes pastors of churches who do not think often enough about ministering to prisoners.

Retired United Methodist Bishop Kenneth L. Carder writes:

> Involvement with prison and jail ministries keeps the pastor focused on life-and-death matters. Leaving the 'free world' and entering the world behind prison walls tends to strip one of pretense and superficial preoccupations.[7]

The most well-known prison ministry organizations are going beyond evangelistic preaching and Bible study to provide classes in substance abuse problems, spousal conflict, anger management, and making peace with the past. These programs can be helpful in preparing offenders for a better way of living before they step out into the world.

Prison Fellowship's InnerChange Freedom Initiative was first started in a Texas prison at Sugar Land, now known as the Carol Vance Unit. Under the capable and long-term leadership of Tommie Dorsett, eligible offenders who enter the program become involved in a rigorous schedule of basically faith-oriented classes that help them to understand themselves and how their criminal actions have hurt others. Offender participants are assigned mentors who are with them at least six months beyond their parole or outright release. The mentors assist them in finding a church home and becoming adjusted to life outside of prison. This eighteen-month program is carried out in several other states.

The Kairos Prison Ministry is a broadly accepted and widely utilized weekend ministry in prisons. Twenty trained volunteers interact one on one with selected offenders from Friday evening until Sunday afternoon.

---

7. Carder, ". . . You Visited Me: The Call to Prison Ministry," 28. Copyright © 2006 Christian Century. Reprinted by permission.

Prisoner participants are greeted with an outpouring of faith and love. They are given letters of encouragement written by volunteers on the outside. Other volunteers provide meals for the participants that include delicious cookies. The Sunday afternoon closing ceremony is like a graduation that loved ones and friends are invited to attend. The program features touching testimonials by those who have been greatly blessed by the ministry of dedicated volunteers.

Gary Whitbeck, the minister who first started visiting Carolyn when she was in the Tarrant County Jail, encouraged her to sign up for an upcoming Kairos event at the Hobby Unit. She spoke favorably to us about the experience and, subsequently, the follow-up Kairos weekends that brought the volunteers back to where the Kairos experience occurred. She wrote afterward to tell us that she never expected "to engage in such a meaningful fellowship inside these walls."

Bridges to Life is an extraordinary program organization founded by John Sage. After the brutal murder of his sister, it took John years to recover. He finally became determined to help crime victims find some measure of peace, while making it possible for criminal offenders to understand the enormity of their offenses and to find their way back to a worthwhile life after serving prison time. Bridges to Life brings incarcerated offenders together with those who have been victims of criminal acts. The offenders learn how their actions caused a world of pain in their victims' lives. Sometimes they hear heartrending accounts of how others have suffered from the deeply personal injury resulting from the murder of a loved one. An important measurement of the success of Bridges to Life is revealed in the minimal number of offender participants who do not return to prison following their release. In addition, it allows crime victims to fulfill a worthwhile purpose in the wake of the crimes that brought suffering to their lives.

The Criminal Justice and Mercy Ministries Committee of the Oklahoma Annual Conference of the United Methodist Church carries out an outstanding church-related program designed to serve the needs of prisoners and their family members. Under the direction of Stan Basler, churches in Oklahoma City, Tulsa, Ardmore, and Lawton, carrying the name "Redemption Church," combine to form a unique fellowship of prisoners, ex-prisoners, their families, and other friends of faith. Through permission granted by the Oklahoma Department of Corrections, church buses and vans driven by volunteers pick up a total of more than 100 eligible prisoners from correctional facilities closest to where each church is located. They participate in study, worship, and fellowship after which they are returned to the prisons. In Oklahoma City, there are Wednesday evening Bible studies and monthly meetings of the United Methodist Men and United Methodist Women made up of prisoners and free world people.

Disciple Bible Study, since 1999, has been taught in seventy different correctional institutions in North Carolina with more than three hundred lay and clergy persons serving as prison volunteers. This accomplishment is attributed to the endorsements the ministry has received from the North Carolina Department of Corrections. Their special teaching ministry, related to the broadly accepted *Disciple Bible Study* series, provides discipleship training for prison inmates along with the added benefit of linking them to local congregations.

The Brothers of St. Dismas, named after the good thief who died on the cross next to Jesus, and the Sisters of St. Mary Magdalene, sponsor an intentional plan of personal transformation for Catholic offenders who become part of an in-prison community of faith. The monitoring chaplain of each prison chapter of the Catholic Dismas/Magdalene Project, Inc. recommends Catholic offenders to a Catholic parish closest to their parole home when they are released. Parish support of prisoners who return home brings to full circle the spirit of love and acceptance first established through the prison connection.

Grace Lutheran Church in River Forest, Illinois, has a group ministry to those in prison that serves as an example of what other churches could do as a special outreach ministry. Their associate minister, Phyllis Kersten, tells about pouring Coca-Cola into plastic cups for the men who lined up on the other side of the bars. She writes:

> What we had to offer, cookies and Coke, was surely inadequate, but I'd like to believe the refreshments represented at least those basics that imprisoned men and women hunger and thirst for—a simple gesture of care; someone who will grieve with us over our losses, over those areas of our past where we messed up; someone who will love us in spite of our brokenness and help us become whole; the opportunity for forgiveness and a new beginning; a oneness that can somehow overcome those things that separate and divide us. We gained a new insight: that Christ's Holy Communion is always, in one way or another, God in Christ reaching through prison bars to us: Christ intervening across those things that would keep us locked in or shut out, to feed us and free us; Christ stretching out

his arms and hands once more to offer us grace and the love of
God and the communion of the Holy Spirit.[8]

Our friend, Murray Batt, a member of the Woodlands United
Methodist Church in Woodlands, Texas, was a co-founder in 1992 of the
East Texas Criminal Justice Ministries. This involvement subsequently
included a specific ministry to prisoners called the Christian Restorative
Justice Mentors Association. As a nonprofit organization, it relies exclu-
sively on volunteers to carry out the Christ-centered work of mentoring
prisoners through their prison time, reentry, and aftercare. In accepting
the word of the Lord, that the fields "are white already to harvest" (John
4:35b, KJV), these good and faithful servants work in harmonious antici-
pation that God will fulfill the promise of bringing his harvest home.

Jim Arnold, a member of First United Methodist in Houston, Texas,
directs Skills for Life: A Prison Ministry. Jim has a passion for bringing
hope and self-esteem to many Texas prisoners by encouraging them to
complete the program of Toastmasters International material and goals
that teach public speaking, personal responsibility, and servant leadership.
The intensive training they receive puts them in a position of advantage
when they are released from prison. Those who attend presentations are
amazed by the poise and professionalism that many formerly speech dis-
advantaged individuals demonstrate.

There is a ministry of kindness to correctional officers who spend
hours dealing with offender problems in ways that often leave them physically and mentally exhausted. For example, there is a man named Jesse
Stewart, a member of Trinity United Methodist Church in Trinity, Texas,
who conducts a personal one-man ministry to the correctional officers of
the Eastham Prison Unit close to where he lives. Once a week, he spends
one to two hours taking bottled water, soda water, and cheese crackers to
those who watch over the offenders. Supported by his church, this form
of discipleship carries an important sign of acceptance to those who are
most often the forgotten ones of prison ministry and, in the process, results in creating a better spirit within the entire facility.

In prisons everywhere there are inmates ministering in faith to each
other. A good example of this is found in a worship service conducted every fifth Sunday by those serving time in the L.V. Hightower Unit for men

8. Kersten, "Reaching Through the Bars," 21. Copyright © 2001 Christian Century.
Reprinted by permission.

near Dayton, Texas. The chaplain, Danny Chapman, explained to me one day about the excitement generated by this service. Offender participants, working within specific guidelines, plan the service beforehand with the chaplain. They sing and play musical instruments. In addition, they pray and witness to their search for peace.

Jorge Antonio Renaud writes about inmate directed faith practices.

> Inmates form informal prayer and Bible study groups. These spontaneous sessions form the foundation of most religious activities in prison. These groups are formed from a deep desire to strengthen those inmates' spiritual values, and their informal structure and setting lends them a strength and validity that many formal meetings lack.[9]

CONNECTING WITH THE PAST

Time held me green and dying
Though I sang in my chains like the sea.[10]

Time exacts its own special punishment in prison through lost memories or ones that are stored away like relics on the dusty shelves of the mind. Relationships that once flourished clear and bright in the springtime of life are reduced to lonely recollections in the winters of prison discontent. Except for the few who are able to sing in their chains, the music of yesteryear is lost in a dream world of irrecoverable pleasures. Lennie Spitale writes:

> The bittersweet joy of memory is the stuff of poetry and ballads. It's that strange mixture of nostalgia and pain that creates the music of the blues and separates mechanical talent from the originals. It is one of prison's primary colors.[11]

A Christmas service in prison, after over seven years of serving time, held special memories of home for Carolyn. During the earliest years of living on the grounds of Holly Hall, the four of us presented a family Christmas program for the residents. In the chapel of Holly Hall, she

---

9. Renaud, *Behind the Walls*, 79.

10. Thomas, "Fern Hill," lines 53–54. Copyright © 1945 by The Trustees for the Copyrights of Dylan Thomas. Reprinted by permission of New Directions Publishing Corporation.

11. Spitale, *Prison Ministry*, 114.

and her brother, Van, as young children, were the featured performers. Marilyn played the organ. I helped with the singing and told a Christmas story. Our annually repeated songs were, "Little Drummer Boy," "Angels We Have Heard on High," and "We Three Kings." The scripture lesson, read by Carolyn, never varied and she knew it by heart. It was Matthew 2:1–2, beginning with the words, "Now when Jesus was born in Bethlehem of Judea in the days of Herod the King . . . "

The offenders who attended the Catholic worship and Bible study assembled for their Christmas Eve service in the area used as a chapel at the William P. Hobby Unit. Deacon Julian Tyboroski, who came regularly for these services, did the scripture readings differently. We had been told by Carolyn that he usually asked for volunteers to read the scripture lessons, but that night, he asked them to take turns, each reading certain marked texts. When Carolyn's turn came, she was startled to see that she was expected to read the same passage from Matthew that she had recited so many times at the Holly Hall Christmas program for the residents. Her eyes filled with tears, she told us, as she struggled to get the words out. Oh, how the memories bless and burn.

VISITING PRISONERS

I can't get away from the words of Jesus found in Matthew 25, "I was in prison and you visited me." When I first started visiting prisoners, I was tempted to think that I might offer them a better understanding of faith in God. Instead, I received a better understanding of prisoners. The short-timers would repeat the words they thought I would be pleased to hear. The "old cons" liked to talk but seemed very frank in what they had to say. While I slipped scripture and prayer into each visit, I was not certain what good, if any, my visits were doing.

At some point, it came to me that not having an overt objective of making the gospel relevant to those I visited created opportunities for special moments to occur, moments uniquely relevant to the gospel. In a climate of acceptance, hints of God as "pure, unbounded love"[12] came from those who had never learned to sing. I prayed more humbly and in different ways. I selected scripture texts that I felt could speak to prison life with a clearer purpose. This objective caused me to think of the story of a banquet in Luke's gospel (14:12–14) where "the poor, the crippled,

12. From the hymn, "Love Divine, All Love's Excelling," written by Charles Wesley.

the lame and the blind," ended up being treated like royalty. They took the places of the customary attendees: friends, relatives, and wealthy neighbors. It was not hard for me to imagine prisoners being included on the new guest list and I thought of them entering the banquet hall singing the words of a hymn written by Fred Pratt Green:

> *Lord, we have come at your own invitation,*
> *Chosen by you, to be counted your friends.*[13]

13. From the hymn, "Lord, We Have Come at Your Own Invitation," written by Fred Pratt Green. Copyright © 1986 Hope Publishing Co., Carol Stream, IL 60188. All rights reserved. Used by permission.

8

What Kind of Justice?

Therefore justice is far from us, and righteousness does not reach us;
we wait for the light, and lo! there is darkness; and for brightness,
but we walk in gloom.

—Isaiah 59:9

MARILYN AND I HAVE heard angry words spoken by family members of those charged with a crime over what is perceived as the lack of justice. Multiple versions of the cry, "It just isn't right!" are voiced repeatedly. They concern a police officer's treatment, the prosecutor's advantage, the judge's attitude, the jury's verdict, and, too often, a lawyer's unfulfilled promise. We learned that a ten-month sentence could be as bitterly lamented as a ten-year sentence and how anger, prejudice, and personal problems work against many of those whose loved ones face criminal charges.

The goal of obtaining equitable justice includes the need of crime victims to feel as if their pain has been addressed compassionately and justly by the court of law responsible for criminal prosecution. Therefore, Christians are called to seek ways through which criminal punishment can be seen as a means of hope for a more just society without imposing further fear, loneliness, and alienation upon those who have suffered from acts of crime. Law enforcement and criminal justice agencies exist because of the need for public safety. Unfortunately, this objective, so necessary for any kind of order to prevail, is not free itself from the problems of human disorder. The public continues to be assured that the punishment perpetrators receive will enable them to rest easier in their homes. At the same time, thousands of unchanged and negatively influenced offenders are being released back upon the streets. Therefore, the question is asked, What Kind of Justice?

The answer to the justice question depends on whether we are speaking on behalf of the secular state or on behalf of the kingdom of God. The law, the police, the courts, and the prisons all represent the earthly order by which we have a certain amount of protection as citizens. They exist as the way we seek to keep our offenses against each other in check. On the other hand, examples of God's justice from the prophets to the teachings of Jesus frame a spiritual order of justice centering in peace, reconciliation, restoration, and forgiveness. While both of these justice ends reflect their own purpose, there are crossover aspects and compromises that Christians accept in order to live in the world.

CRIMINAL JUSTICE CONCERNS

Justice is turned back and righteousness stands at a distance;
for truth stumbles in the public square and uprightness cannot enter.

—Isaiah 59:14

Justice is turned back when the wrong person is charged and convicted, when law enforcement officials forcibly extract confessions from a frightened and defenseless suspect, when false testimony is secured from unreliable witnesses, and when there is inaccurate scientific testing in crime laboratories. In addition, justice is not served when prison sentences are handed down that punish far more than the crime deserves.

The problem of measuring guilt goes beyond the criminal action. As Christopher Marshall suggests, "Moral guilt is not coterminous with legal guilt. Moral culpability cannot be quantified objectively. It varies from person to person and depends on innumerable circumstances."[1] In the rush to judgment, it is likely to be forgotten that individual "choices are constrained by environmental circumstances, and it is naïve, if not dishonest, to speak of crime solely in terms of personal free will."[2]

Criminal justice systems and the punishment they impose cannot change the way life in cities and communities draws individuals into extreme forms of behavior. Neither can they heal the wounds of mind

1. Marshall, *Beyond Retribution*, 114.
2. Ibid., 112.

and spirit carried by those who have been violated by criminal acts. They can only isolate and punish according to the terms of the established authority. Considering the difference between actions that are labeled as criminal and the broader problem of sin, it seems better, in the light of apparent injustices, to ask the psalmist's question, "If you, O Lord, should mark iniquities, Lord, who could stand?" (Ps 131:3).

Carolyn's experience in the Harris County Jail includes witnessing the outcome of a particular decision made by the local criminal justice system.

> Vera was arrested for theft and given 10-years probation. She came back to the tank after going to court and was to be released that evening. As a part of her probation terms she was assigned to do specific community service. It was close to Christmas and her assignment was to buy a toy and take it to the 'Toys for Tots' drive by two o'clock p.m. the next day. She dutifully announced to all of us that she would have to go out and steal a toy in order to comply with her probation because, of course, she didn't have any money with which to buy a toy. In this case, she maintained that if she had money she wouldn't have been stealing in the first place. Sure enough, within eight hours Vera was back in jail after being re-arrested for shoplifting in a toy store. One must certainly question the 'system' in this case as well as in many others. What good does it do to arrest people and keep them in jail for a matter of days? This is certainly not going to make any major changes in a person's way of life.

While defense attorneys may work hard to obtain sympathy for their clients, the criminal courts do not, in any substantive way, assess the reasons that exist behind the crimes for which a criminal judgment is sought. They are seldom able to make allowances for crimes that result from basic human needs. The background of tragedy associated with much criminal activity is not usually considered except, in some instances, during the punishment phase of a trial. Learning what possesses individuals who injure other people or deprive them of their property is the subject of studies undertaken apart from the arena where guilt or innocence is decided.

Howard Zehr, a Mennonite consultant on criminal justice, relates how the prevailing system can fail both offender and victim.

> The legal concept of guilt that guides the justice process is technical and abstracted from experience. This makes it easier for offenders to avoid accepting personal responsibility for their behavior. It also

frustrates victims, who find it difficult to match the legal description of the event with their own experience. Both 'victim' and 'offender' are forced to speak the language of the 'system,' to define their reality in its terms instead of their own.[3]

Christ's victory over death does not change the limited systems that deal with criminal acts and the errors and omissions that regularly occur in the name of justice. It does establish that the ultimate authority belongs to God and that Christians everywhere will continue to witness in their worship to the power of love even as they witness in their work to the importance of truth and honor in the public arena.

RESTORATIVE JUSTICE

Restorative justice is a concept, based on our human understanding of God's covenant design for peace, that focuses on the righting of wrongs that occur as the result of criminal acts. It borrows from indigenous cultures, such as those represented by Native Americans that view crimes as acts that break relationships we have with each other and with the larger realities of life. As opposed to the design of retribution that uses punishment as a way to even the score, restorative justice seeks to heal relationships damaged by wrong-doing. Howard Zehr writes:

> In today's justice, all action is hierarchical, from the top down. The state acts on the offender, with the victim on the sidelines. Restorative justice would put victim and offender at the center, helping to decide what is to be done about what has happened. Thus the definition of accountability would change. Instead of 'paying a debt to society' by experiencing punishment, accountability would mean undertaking and taking responsibility for what has been done and taking action to make things right. Instead of owing an abstract debt to society, paid in an abstract way by experiencing punishment, the offender would owe a debt to the victim, to be repaid in a concrete way.[4]

Ronnie Earle, a Texas District Attorney from Austin's Travis County, soon to be retired after twenty-seven years of service in that position, gave a major speech at Rice University in Houston on April 10, 2002. In that speech, Earle described our justice system as one handed down from

---

3. Zehr, *Changing Lenses*, 72.
4. Zehr, "Retributive Justice, Restorative Justice," 16.

William the Conqueror who used it to control the population by asking: Who did it? What law did they break? How can we punish them? Earle went on to explain:

> This system removed the dispute from the community by taking ownership of peace itself and making crime a disturbance of the King's peace. To this day, indictments in Texas end with the words, 'Against the peace and dignity of the State,' with the state the lineal descendent of the king. The point of law was upholding the authority of the king. The point was not the victim and not the community.[5]

Restorative justice, which is victim-centered, asks, concerning each crime: What is the harm? What needs to be done to repair it? Who is responsible for the harm? Many Christians today support ministries of relief and recovery for those affected by crime but that do not compromise the purpose prisons serve in holding men and women responsible for the harm they have caused.

A well-known proponent of restorative justice ministries is a native Texan by the name of Emmett Solomon who, after serving for thirty years as a prison chaplain, the last seven as State Director of Chaplain Services, currently serves as President of the Restorative Justice Ministries Network headquartered in Huntsville, Texas. He possesses an extensive knowledge of criminal justice systems and a clear understanding of what incarceration does to those who suffer from retributive punishment. His soft manner belies the passion that burns within him for a cause often misunderstood and ignored by the general public.

Restorative justice, as taught and practiced by people like Emmett Solomon, includes much of what is called prison ministry. However, it is much broader in scope, supporting programs that help victims of crime, children of offenders, and prison personnel, along with making contact with state legislators concerning prison reform. Conferences sponsored by the Restorative Justice Ministries Network, held in cities across Texas, bring together representatives of various agencies and ministries that share with attendees news, information, and inspiration related to how faith in God can help restore hope to prisoners and those who care for them.

---

5. A portion of the speech Ronnie Earle delivered at Rice University in Houston on April 10, 2002. Permission granted by Earle in a personal email reply received on December 1, 2005.

Sadly, many who return to crowded cities from prison do not experience the joys of being restored to freedom. Unable to find a job or a place to call home, they return to where their living expenses are paid and they are not asked to leave. The weight of their plight is known by God and sorrowfully acknowledged by those who call out to God to help them. We hear the urgency of this call in the words of "Where Cross the Crowded Way of Life," a hymn written by Frank Mason North:

> *O Master, from the mountainside,*
> *make haste to heal these hearts of pain;*
> *Among these restless throngs abide,*
> *O tread the city's streets again.*

—fifth stanza

There are signs in Houston, Texas, of an important breakthrough in dealing with drug-related crimes. Some judges are giving their own time to set up duly constituted court hearings along with carefully monitored assessments of individuals charged with possession or usage of drugs. The brightening of this one area of criminal justice is consistent with our call as Christians to serve the present age. So, whether it is family group counseling or drug courts, Christians give thanks as they affirm the truth that "Christ's whole life was a sacrifice that takes away sin in the only way in which sin can really be taken away, and that is by making the sinner actually better."[6]

Based on "The Magnificat" (Luke 1:46–55), Jan Johnson uses the song of Mary to weave the qualities of justice and mercy together. She writes:

> Mary's song . . . provides a clue about how to live out radical justice steeped with tender mercy. It is this: offering a voice to those who have been rendered voiceless. To speak on their behalf retrains us to spend ourselves for justice while flowing with mercy instead of just getting mad (merciless justice) or rescuing indiscriminately (justiceless mercy).[7]

God's people, in increasing numbers, are addressing the needs of crime victims, offenders, and the community through a combination of boldness and submissiveness. They are bold in confidently entering places

6. Gorringe, *God's Just Vengeance*, 214. Reprinted by permission of Cambridge University Press.

7. Johnson, "Mary's Merciful Song of Justice," 40.

under siege from the *powers*, and submissive to *God* who, through Jesus, has already obtained the victory. When we affirm a hope based on nothing less than the righteousness of Jesus, we are not nearly as possessed by budgets, buildings, or bureaucracies as ways to meet what is described as a criminal justice crisis. I am reminded by Stanley Hauerwas that we "live after the only crisis that matters, which means that Jesus has given us all the time in the world to visit him in the prisons of this world."[8]

PRISON PUNISHMENT

The punishment inflicted upon offenders through serving time in prison does not reform or rehabilitate. Neither does it serve as a deterrent to committing future crimes. In fact, prison punishment is sometimes accepted as a rite of passage for young people who enter prison from communities overrun by crime and violence.

The punishment prison inflicts does not end when the debt of prison time has been paid. Instead, it haunts the lives of ex-offenders who have been released but who cannot shake off the negative image of prison. A large number are unable to find a way to live law-abiding and self-supporting lives. The hurt of broken homes and severed relationships continues to haunt those who have spent far too much time in prison. And yet, in prisons throughout the land, there are increasing numbers of God's people who offer hope as agents of mercy to those who are being punished, sometimes unjustly. They dedicate with prayer each prisoner's application for citizenship in God's peaceable kingdom.

The greatest positive potential for some of those who endure prison punishment rests with the kind of shame that leads to accepting responsibility for the harm they have done to other human beings. Prisoners who suffer guilt and remorse for their offenses are the most likely to hear the call to come home. Carolyn's experiences through jail and prison time were punishing reminders to her of the years of freedom that had been lost to her. She wrote these words to us:

> To me there is no punishment like remorse. It is agonizing to stare
> at the ruins of my actions from a distance and not be able to start
> actively working to repair and rebuild these ruins in a way that will
> be meaningful to all who were affected by my criminal activity. I feel
> the punishment of remorse when there is a report of danger or foul

8. Hauerwas, *Matthew*, 212.

weather where my loved ones reside . . . I can't call to hear a reassuring voice. The only voices I hear here are those that carry the hoots, cackles, and screams of the others here with me and the voice that resonates in my mind saying: 'Because of your actions you can't call and check on them. Because of your actions you are not there if they need you . . .' That is a glimpse of the agony of remorse.

Remorse over having done wrong also comes from remembering the crime clearly enough to feel the hurt others have experienced because of it. Consequently, restoration means accepting responsibility for wrongs that have been done (the confession of sin) and, subsequently, being brought back to the Lord's Table (tasting "afresh the calm of sin forgiven"). The gift of securing a firmer grasp of God's love often involves a heartrending experience. Carolyn said it well when she commented later: "I had to be brought to my knees." Through aching hearts and bruised knees, God's wayward children have the opportunity to relearn their true names and return home. Stanley Hauerwas explains it this way:

> To be punished as a Christian is to be called home so that we may
> be reunited with the community of forgiven sinners called church
> and, thus, reconciled with our own life.[9]

As the years passed, Carolyn continued to worry about how she would ever be able to compensate us for all we had been through because of her days of trouble. Gary Whitbeck, as God's special emissary, with constant faithfulness and skill, helped her through the punishment of guilt she carried and encouraged her participation in the special ministry of Kairos. Marilyn and I, meanwhile, continued to be surrounded by witnesses to how the love of God manifests itself through friendship and prayer.

9. Hauerwas, *Performing the Faith*, 199.

CAPITAL PUNISHMENT

*Let the groans of the prisoners come before you; according to
your great power preserve those doomed to die.*

—Psalm 79:11

Capital punishment, as it is carried out in the United States, is the subject
of widespread controversy. Supporters of the death penalty cite the importance of exacting vengeance against those who wantonly take the life
of another human being. They insist that the maximum penalty should
be paid in order to help compensate family members whose loved ones
have been murdered and, at the same time, to satisfy the broader public
expectation of justice. On the other hand, the arguments most often presented in opposition to the death penalty include its failure as a deterrent,
inequities in sentencing, lack of alternative sentencing for the mentally
ill, the cruel and unusual punishment involved, its greater expense to the
state, widespread negative impact upon society, and possibility of execut-
ing someone who is innocent.

While our life in Christ cannot bring an end to capital punishment, it
can reveal to the world how serving a risen savior robs death of its power.
We are called through the strength of faith in God to disown the act of
murder (no matter how or by whom it is carried out) and to minister in
whatever ways are possible to those who suffer from the wounds such
tragic circumstances inflict. Clearly, our praying and singing is an exercise
of devotion that builds up the faith and, as a result, resists the power of sin
and death. According to Walter Brueggemann, ,

> All these prayers and songs speak of the intervening action of
> God to give life in a world where death seems to have the best and
> strongest way. The songs are not about the "natural" outcome of
> trouble, but about the decisive *transformation* made possible by
> this God who causes new life where none seems possible.[10]

CONFESSION AND FORGIVENESS

Many who commit crimes find it hard to honestly confess their guilt, to
express truthfully and uniquivocally what they have done. Many will re-

10. Brueggemann, *Spirituality of the Psalms*, 49.

fuse to acknowledge their responsibility for other people being hurt or robbed, and some of them will even talk as if their rights have been violated. Bo Lozoff, an advocate of prisoners and their counselor over many years, agrees with this finding.

> I've noticed something for years having to do with the way a lot of prisoners talk about their lives. For example, I can be sitting with a guy who just blew three people away with a .38, and he'll describe it like 'I was convicted of three counts of murder.' It's always in the passive tense of what was done to him, rather than the active tense of what he did. 'They convicted me, they sentenced me, they violated my parole, etc.'[11]

Many offenders spend hours with family members and friends seeking to make their crimes seem less offensive or, in many instances, to explain how they were framed. Some of this evasiveness comes from the idea that a confession of guilt renders the perpetrator defenseless, weighed down by the burden of appearing either despicable or weak. They determine that it is nobler to protest their innocence, relishing any sympathy they might gain because of the alleged injustice they have suffered. There are those who have hurt others by their criminal acts who seek to avoid conversation about what they have done because they are so ashamed of their deeds. Others, through repeatedly embellished testimonies and the passage of time, come to believe that what they are revealing is actually the truth. A quote from Friedrich Nietzsche illustrates the kind of emotional response that generates forgetfulness.

> 'I have done that,' says my memory. 'I cannot have done that,' says my pride, and remains inexorable. Eventually—memory yields.[12]

We all act from self-interest at times by "spinning" the truth to our advantage. By the same token, a certain amount of selective remembering often comes from both sides during a criminal trial. While the greatest amount of sympathy and concern rests with the victims of crimes, it only follows that victims, in reacting to what they have suffered at the hands of perpetrators, in certain instances may present an exaggerated truth or one that leaves out something important to the decisions the court must make.

---

11. Lozoff, *We're All Doing Time*, 173.
12. Nietzsche, *Beyond Good and Evil*, 79.

Christopher Marshall writes about how repentance is often scorned by offenders and, as a result, the chance of being forgiven is minimized.

> . . . it is possible for recalcitrant offenders to place themselves in a position of such inner resistance to grace that repentance becomes subjectively impossible and God's forgiveness remains unappropriated . . . It is not that there are certain kinds of *offenses* that do not deserve forgiveness. (Forgiveness is never deserved!) Rather, there are certain kinds of *offenders* who run the risk of so stubbornly repudiating forgiving grace that they make restoration of relationship with God effectively impossible, since relational renewal always requires both parties to be willing. They condemn themselves to unforgiveness; they remain wedded to sin, which brings alienation and death.[13]

Forgiveness is rejected by many of those who have had a criminal act committed against them or a member of their family. They cannot abide the thought of a forgiveness that has the result of making the criminal seem less inhuman and the crime they have committed seem less offensive. As a result, they are caught within a web of anger and grief from which they cannot free themselves. Fixed in a position of misery and pain, their feelings of victimization reach a point where recovery seems impossible.

Nothing less than the love of God will suffice to bring healing to the victims of terrible crimes. This kind of love, coming from the dwelling place of light, is available to those who gradually surrender their fears to the kind of justice that restores hope in God. A lesson from the word of God, found in 1 John, offers hope in the love that in not letting us go helps to banish the fears that cling to us.

> *There is no fear in love, but perfect love casts out fear;*
> *for fear has to do with punishment,*
> *and whoever fears has not reached perfection in love.*

—1 John 4:18

What kind of justice? Surely, we are called to uphold the kind of justice that seeks healing, reconciliation, and peace. As God's people, we are pointed toward the forms of justice that work to keep the disabled, the poor, and the mentally ill from being treated in ways that limit possibilities for their recovery and push them deeper into the hopeless cycle of re-

---

13. Marshall, *Beyond Retribution*, 94–95.

turning again and again to prison. Restorative justice offers hope in God's love even for those who have no hope of ever being released from prison. Such justice is more personally demanding but far more satisfying in the long run than the justice that continues to condemn, divide, and stir up more hatred, conflict, and grief. As Christopher Marshall summarizes:

> Because Jesus personally incarnates the moral and political message he proclaims about the inbreaking of God's justice, simply to hear the story of Jesus is already to receive moral instruction, while to emulate the example of Jesus is to imitate God.[14]

The promises of God are finally dependent upon our obedience and are part of an everlasting covenant of faith.

> *Thus says the Lord:*
> *Maintain justice, and do what is right,*
> *for soon my salvation will come,*
> *and my deliverance be revealed.*

—Isaiah 56:1

14. Ibid., 259.

9

Release/Deliverance

Pilate, wanting to release Jesus,
addressed them again;

—Luke 23:20

Deliverance belongs to the Lord;
may your blessing be upon your people!

—Psalm 3:8

THE WORDS, "RELEASE" AND "deliverance," may be used interchangeably. "Release," it seems to me, best defines an offender's desire and a family's hope regarding the end of prison time. "Deliverance," on the other hand, seems more compatible with the idea of being brought out from the kind of bondage that prison represents. More than permission to leave, it carries the hint of a spiritually assisted separation. When the agency of release works primarily within the terms of each prisoner's confinement, there are feelings of excitement and relief over being able to walk out into the free world. But when the agency of release includes the work of the Lord, there is an increase of joy that comes from having received the gift of deliverance.

RELEASE

Joseph, in Genesis 39, is thrown into prison after being falsely accused by the wife of the Pharaoh's guard captain of seeking intimacy with her. Fortunately, for Joseph, he gained the favor of the chief jailer who trusted him with caring for the other prisoners. Then, in the fortieth chapter, Joseph finds the chief cupbearer and the chief baker of the king in prison with him. Having heard of his gift of being able to interpret dreams, both the chief cupbearer and the chief baker seek Joseph's interpretation of the dreams they have had. After interpreting the cupbearer's dream favorably, Joseph makes this request of him:

> *But remember me when it is well with you;*
> *please do me the kindness to make mention of me to Pharaoh,*
> *and so get me out of this place.*

—Genesis 40:14

The prospect of getting out of prison figures prominently in the lives of prisoners and those who support them. Release, as a door opening to the highway home, brings unbounded joy to fathers and mothers. The same is true, in another way, for spouses who have gone through so much by themselves, often as the sole supporters of their children. Some of those being released from prison will have been delivered from the forces of darkness that sent them to prison in the first place. Others, sadly, will be released with unresolved problems that lead, in far too many instances, to additional prison time.

The sight of prisoners actually being released from various locations throughout the country is viewed with mixed feelings. There is gladness associated with those who have family members to meet them at their release point and supporters to meet them at church. There is a sadness associated with those who have been locked up for many years who are put on a bus and dropped off at city bus stations without anyone there to meet them. As a regular recipient of Emmett Solomon's email messages sent to Restorative Justice friends and associates, I was interested in his letter of December 4, 2003. There, he described the men just released from prison at the Huntsville Unit who wait at the bus station for a ride back to their communities.

> Large numbers of old men are there, many with 20 years of incarceration under their belts. Another sizeable number are those who have served 30 or more years. These people have been left largely incapacitated with a life frittered away in prison. It makes me wonder, 'Would not there have been a better way of dealing with these men. Might the half-million dollars spent on a man to keep him locked up for 30-plus years have been better spent in some other effort?' Yes, some were there for heinous crimes. Yet other nonviolent men had done their life sentences on the installment plan: two years, five years, ten years, and then finally twenty years. This imprisonment is why restorative measures are so important.

Restorative justice promotes healing. Our traditional system produces suffering. As I look into the sad eyes of these 'lost souls' I see the walking dead.

Prisoners are granted release from prison for one of four specific reasons.

1. A pardon is granted to certain prisoners in very unusual cases. The country's president or the state's governor may grant a pardon. While a pardon generally exempts a convicted offender from further punishment, it may in some instances be partial, excluding only a part of the punishment.[1]

2. Release may be granted in instances where new evidence is found that exonerates the one originally convicted of the offense.

3. Release on parole is an option many states allow.

4. Outright release upon the completion of a sentence is the most common way out of prison.

Release on parole represents the best opportunity to get out of prison before one's sentence has been completed. Such release is based upon the idea that the successful reintegration of the offender into the community is hastened when the offender serves the final portion of his sentence in the community under the supervision of a parole officer. Parole serves as an incentive of hope for those who long to be free of the restrictive life they endure.

A movement for the abolition of parole gained favorable attention in 1977. Senator Edward Kennedy sponsored a bill to change the federal criminal code to stop paroles entirely. He argued the point that, in addition to the possible abuse of discretion at parole hearings, the existence of a parole system could encourage judges to favor lengthy sentences. This, he believed, would make communities think they were being "tough on

---

1. There is a commingling of terminology with other unusual methods of release including commutation of sentence, time cut, clemency, reprieve, and medical reprieve. The parole board may recommend the commutation of a sentence (reduction in time) to the governor, who is the only person authorized to commute a sentence. Such a request must be accompanied by a recommendation from at least two of the trial parties involved (trial judge, sheriff, or district attorney). A specific remainder sentence is suggested and the parties must agree that this sentence is appropriate. A medical reprieve may be granted when an offender is terminally ill or has a condition for which treatment is not available from the prison's medical contractor. However, if the "outside" treatment is successful, the offender is then re-incarcerated.

crime" even while the judges expected that parole boards would ultimately release offenders early. In 1984, parole from federal prisons ended and a number of state prison systems followed suit.

State statutes define state crimes and Congress defines federal crimes. Cases cannot be tried on an appeal from a state court to a federal court, except to the U.S. Supreme Court, and then only when a constitutional right is involved. A large number of the cases brought to federal courts by state prisoners fit those courts because the inmates allege that their federal rights have been violated.

Offenders appearing before parole board members should be ready to present three key points that underscore their worthiness to be released on parole.

1. They should speak honestly about their criminal offenses and give evidence of remorse for having committed them.

2. They should tell the parole board what steps they have taken to improve their mind, their attitude, and their behavior. Those who are serving time for drug related crimes should convey a purpose and a design for remaining drug free.

3. They should project a positive self-image and give evidence of how they intend to be self-supportive if they are released on parole. If offenders who appear before a parole board show the slightest indication of being a threat to public safety, denial of their parole is a foregone conclusion. This is what causes the numerous parole rejections officially labeled "the nature of the crime." However, the majority of denials are the result of individual assessments that not enough "calendar time" has been served relative to the offender's sentence.

A preliminary letter to the parole board from the offender is important. Although it is suggested that letters be limited to five type-written, double-spaced pages, handwritten letters are also accepted. Since the majority of offenders do not have access to a typewriter, concentration should be on legibility and adequate spacing of the handwritten letter. A list of what should be included in the letter follows:

1. A summary of the offender's case (do not re-try the case), the offender's recognition of his/her problem, and an acceptance of responsibility.

2. A background and history of the offender from birth forward (1 page maximum).

3. Institutional adjustment (what the offender has done with his/her time, listing significant changes, classes taken, etc.).

4. A parole plan that includes basic information such as living arrangements, transportation, and job promises, and if there are no promises, any reasonable prospects.

5. A Summary of the offender's self-assessment that supports his/her release on parole.

Those who offer advice to family members and friends about how to put parole support information together recommend that only a few well-written letters be sent to the parole board. Support letters, including one from a potential employer, should identify the offender by name and number, reveal how the supporter knows the offender, and what they know about the offender that substantiates belief in their recommendation of release on parole. Each letter should reveal the kind of assistance the family member or friend who is writing will provide if the offender is granted parole. In their letter, family members can include a request for an interview with the parole board member responsible for reviewing their loved one's case. There is general agreement that interviews have only a marginal chance of influencing a favorable parole decision. A family should request an interview if they feel strongly about being able to put forth a strong case on behalf of their loved one. An interview does provide the parole board representative an opportunity to evaluate the supportive intent and capability of the family.

Texas parole guidelines allow the parole board to vote what is called a "set-off." A "set-off" is parole parlance for setting a later date for the next parole opportunity, usually one, two, three, or five years. At any review time, a "serve-all" may be voted. This means that the entire sentence must be completed in prison. There are often very different decisions voted in cases that seem very much alike. Sometimes parole board members who speak at inmate family meetings explain in general terms why this can happen. There are variables it seems in making parole decisions, including an offender's age, criminal history, number of previous arrests/convictions, and the testimony of victims and supporters. In addition, there is a wide range of voting options, (e.g., parole granted at a future date is sometimes dependent upon completing a particular class or rehabilitation program).

A date may be arbitrarily set for another review, or additional reviews may be denied. In Texas, three parole panel members vote on each case. A parole panel may vote against a mandatory supervision release if they do not think the offender's record of good behavior is sufficient to inspire confidence that he or she would not be a threat to public safety. Finally, we have heard parole board members admit to a workload that severely limits the time they have to study individual cases.

The denial of parole can discourage offenders who have made substantial positive changes while serving their sentences. No matter how much the risk assessment tools used by the parole board show favorable conditions for release, they may have no affect on how the board reaches its final decision. A first-time offender who has been a model prisoner and who seems to have everything in place for the best possible reentry conditions cannot be certain of receiving a favorable vote.

I would not want anyone to conclude, based on what I have described, that their loved one will never be approved for parole. I encourage those who face the parole review of a family member or friend to do everything possible to influence the parole board. No matter what happens, the good things an offender has done, along with how clearly he or she has demonstrated change, will not in some way go unrewarded and they may contribute to a different parole decision at the next review.

The thought of Carolyn coming up for parole, after serving five years of her sentence, kept Marilyn and I searching for the best way to present her case to representatives of the parole board. In reaching the decision to do all the preliminary work ourselves, we were aware of the fact that first-time parole reviews on similar cases were hardly ever voted for release. We learned a lot from speakers, some of them parole attorneys, at chapter meetings of the Texas Inmate Families Association. We put together support letters, pictures, a job offer, and the assurance that we would provide Carolyn's housing and transportation. Our packet of material was more than sufficient to cover the most important points. The personal letter Carolyn wrote was, in itself, a remarkable testimony to how much she deserved serious parole consideration.

I wrote a letter to the regional office where Carolyn's parole file would be sent and requested that Marilyn and I, along with her brother, Van, and Gary Whitbeck, be granted an interview with the parole board member assigned to her case. A short time afterward, I started calling the parole board office once a week to ask if Carolyn's file had been received from

Austin. In addition to that question, I repeatedly reminded the administrative assistant who answered the phone that my written request was for four of us to be present for the interview. Finally, on the day of our appointment, Marilyn and I met Van and Gary at a McDonald's restaurant in Gatesville, Texas. After we visited briefly, Gary offered a prayer and we made our way to the regional parole office. We felt fortunate to have been granted an interview and that four of us were being allowed to speak for Carolyn.

We entered the parole office on time and did not have to wait long in the outer area before being directed into the meeting room by the person I assumed to be the administrative assistant. The parole board member came in and offered his hand to each one of us. Except for a few brief glances, he did not look at me during my opening statement. This made it harder for me to speak with confidence that I was being heard. I even wondered, as he looked down at the papers in front of him, if he was studying our daughter's file for the first time. Marilyn, Van, and Gary were given the opportunity to make brief statements in support of Carolyn's parole request.

The parole board member we met in Gatesville that day was obviously a well-educated, experienced representative of the Texas parole system. He surprised us by using the word "aberration" to describe Carolyn's trouble, and further, in a voice that revealed a hint of concern, he asked about Carolyn's health. After Marilyn described Carolyn's health problems that, at the time, were not terribly serious, I was taken off guard when he looked at me and asked if I would "sum up." I was unable to say anything at that moment except that we just wanted her out.

At the conclusion of the interview, we followed the parole board member out of the room. As he turned away from us in the hall, he gave a dismissive wave of his hand toward the door through which we had entered the building. When we were outside, we expressed our feelings briefly, told Gary goodbye after offering our thanks to him for being with us, and drove back home.

After months of careful preparation for Carolyn's parole review, we had allowed a ray of hope for her release to slip into our thinking. That hope was dimmed significantly by our interview with the parole board member. Later that month, giving the three-panel board time to cast their vote, I called the Gatesville office of the Texas Board of Pardons and Paroles and was shocked to learn that our daughter had been given a three-year set-off. It would be three more years before the board would again consider her parole.

Carolyn did not express bitterness when we visited with her the following weekend. She seemed more concerned about us and how we were dealing with her lengthy set-off. We discussed the negative decision openly and with love and consideration for each other. She told us about adjusting her daily routine as a way of simulating a fresh start on whatever amount of time remained for her to serve.

Messages of comfort and assurance helped us to move beyond the judgment that Carolyn had not been punished enough. The first letter Carolyn received after we conveyed the disappointing news to faithful friends, many of them related in special ways to the church, was from Bishop Alfred Norris of the Texas Annual Conference of the United Methodist Church. A card from St. Luke's, with signatures of the staff members, helped Carolyn realize how much they cared for her and for her family. We would have to wait longer for her release from prison but were nonetheless thankful for the special gift of deliverance that had already begun to invest her life with hope for the future. We felt sure that Carolyn would not allow the disappointment of parole rejection to slow her freedom initiative. A letter to us from Gary Whitbeck, who would continue his faithful visitation, closed with the words, "God will not abandon Carolyn. Look forward to the grand celebration we will have when she is finally released!"

Sadly, large numbers of people walk the streets following their release from prison with nowhere to go and no resources to help them survive. They have been physically released from prison but they have not been delivered from prison's negative influence upon their lives. As a result, they are met by one dead end after another. Their condition, making life outside of prison seem hopeless, is the reason so many of them return to jail and prison. The church, with its belief in a God who welcomes, pardons, and sets free, is seeking greater understanding about those who might have a chance if they could only receive the right kind of assistance.

One established assistance program called First Contact, started by First Baptist Church in Huntsville, Texas, provides information and encouragement to those who are about to be released from prison. The program trains volunteers from a number of different churches to meet with offenders at the Walls Unit in Huntsville (for the men) and the Gatesville Unit (for the women) on the evening or morning before their release. They visit with the men and women and obtain information about where they will be going. If they indicate a church preference, contacts are made with churches that have promised to reach out to them following their release. A brochure is given to those about to leave prison. In it, helpful advice and information is offered, including telephone numbers to locate Alcoholics Anonymous and Narcotics Anonymous classes.[2]

Another valuable release assistance program was started several years ago through St. James United Methodist Church in Montgomery, Alabama. Kate, an ex-offender who spoke at the church, held the audience in rapt attention as she told of being released from prison. Janice Shaw Crouse writes about it:

> Most of the women listening to Kate were surprised to learn that while job training programs, rehabilitation services, and other special programs offered within the prison are effective, each released inmate is on her own when she walks through the prison gates into the outside world. Each woman is given tan slacks and a white shirt along with a ten-dollar check and a one-way bus ticket. That's all—no money, no job, no identification, and no place to go—wearing what is easily recognizable in the region as standard prison release garb.[3]

In response to Kate's story, the women of St. James, under the leadership of Kim Bullard, started a mission project to assist the women who are released from prison to the outside world. The St. James women converted an old barn into a stylish clothing boutique called Kate's Closet and stocked it with women's clothing and accessories. Volunteers greet each woman released from prison with a hug and a smile and then assist them with an amazing shopping experience. In addition to a complete clothing change, they are given a makeover and, before they leave, they receive a prayer, a Bible, a promise book, and a wrapped basket of hygiene items. Women released from prison who go through Kate's Closet are fortunate. They resume their lives outside of prison with good feelings about the kind of acceptance they received as they left the prison.

Men and women who are serving long prison sentences often stop thinking about going home and, at the same time, people who live on the outside find it troubling that prisoners might one day be released. While prisoners do not live beyond the miracle of God's redeeming love, a wary

2. The First Contact ministry has been expanded in Texas to include women who are released from prison in Gatesville, Texas, as well as within some of the state jails where short-term offenders are released.

3. Crouse, "Finding Hope in Kate's Closet," lines 15–21. Used by permission of Janice Shaw Crouse, Ph.D., Senior Fellow, The Beverly LaHaye Institute.

public will inevitably view them as a threat to peace and tranquility. Many of these individuals have been in prison so long they will find it difficult to live in the outside world. Emmett Solomon notes a major obstacle that released prisoners face:

> Keeping a person in the 'child role' for years and then one day opening the door to society and instructing the prisoner to go and be a good man or good woman makes no sense at all.[4]

Nonprofit organizations are being formed with the objective of helping men and women who lack support to meet the challenges of getting a fresh start in life when they are released from prison. Allen Rice, a man motivated by personal experience and a background of Christian discipleship, founded an organization called SpiritKey to assist men and women upon their release from prison. The guidelines he established for this ministry are: (1) to meet personally with each one who is seeking help; (2) to offer them necessities but not money; (3) to require discipline and accountability. Allen is wise to point out that not everyone who seeks help will be successful. This is important for understanding how hard it is to pull anyone out of a long-established pattern of negative dependency

A large number of men and women, whose first prison sentence was connected to substance abuse, will fall into a similar pattern of drug connected criminal activity following their release. I once visited a man in prison who, because of a drug problem, was in and out of prison three times before finally accepting the terms of freedom. Another man who I visited for a long period of time was released on parole and obtained an excellent job that he described to me as his "life." Sadly, almost five years following his release and in ways he chose not to reveal to us, he allowed his success to be compromised, was taken advantage of, and lost his job. He called me from what he described as a "bad place," reflecting deep remorse for having "let me down." I prayed for him over the phone and urged him to seek help. The next evening he called to tell me that he had checked himself into a hospital where he would be undergoing treatment.

4. I received this email message from Emmett Solomon on May 5, 2008, as a friend and associate of his Restorative Justice Network.

DELIVERANCE

You are a hiding place for me; you preserve me from trouble;
You surround me with glad cries of deliverance.

—Psalm 32:7

When the Hebrew slaves were spared from being killed or captured by the Pharaoh's army by slipping through the parted waters of the Red Sea, a song from the lips of Miriam, accompanied by a group of women playing tambourines, celebrated their dramatic escape. Many years later, the captive people in Babylon remembered Jeremiah's promise of deliverance from the punishment of their long exile. His word from the Lord, written upon their hearts, was:

Only when Babylon's seventy years are completed will I visit you,
and I will fulfill to you my promise and bring you back (to your home).
For surely I know the plans I have for you, says the Lord,
plans for your welfare and not for harm, to give you a future with hope.

—Jeremiah 29:10–11 (NRSV)

When Isaiah heard God's directions to "comfort his people,"[5] he responded by sending a message of calm assurance across the miles to where the captives went about their daily routine.

Speak tenderly to Jerusalem,
and cry to her that she has served her term,
that her penalty is paid, that she has received
from the Lord's hand double for all her sins.

—Isaiah 40:2

These "people of God" did not understand at first what they were hearing. Some were too slow of heart to believe the announcement of their long-awaited deliverance. Some were satisfied with being quasi-citizens of the land into which so many of their people were brought as captives so many years before. Others remembered what they had been told

---

5. The long forward movement of time and the different style of writing between the end of the thirty-ninth chapter of Isaiah and the beginning of the fortieth chapter is generally accepted as coming from the pen of a "Second Isaiah." It echoes God's call to "bring out the prisoners from the dungeon, from the prison those who sit in darkness" (Isa 42:7b).

by their fathers and mothers about why they were living in a land that was not really their own. One of Israel's poets prepared, as a lesson for future generations, a summary of what happened to the chosen ones as a result of their disaffection and disloyalty to God.

> *Some sat in darkness and gloom,*
> *prisoners in affliction and in irons,*
> *for they had rebelled against the words of God,*
> *and spurned the counsel of the Most High.*
> *Their hearts were bowed down with hard labor;*
> *they fell down with no one to help.*

—Psalm 107:10–11

Those who returned to their homeland told the story that Israel would forever remember:

> *Then they cried to the Lord in their trouble,*
> *and he saved them from their distress;*
> *he brought them out of darkness and gloom,*
> *and broke their bonds asunder.*
> *Let them thank the Lord for his steadfast love,*
> *for his wonderful works to humankind!*
> *For he shatters the doors of bronze,*
> *and cuts in two the bars of iron.*

—Psalm 107:13–16

Marilyn and I reached a point where we were relieved of any doubt over Carolyn's state of mind. Her deliverance from whatever controlled her life for a time became evident to us. In possession of "new lenses," as she expressed it, she was able to look back and recognize the wrong turns she had taken. She was also able to look forward where, with clear vision, she remained focused on the highway paved with freedom and honor that stretched out before her. She sent us this prayer:

May I have time to surround my family with the kind of love such as they demonstrated toward me even when I was at my worst. May I do something good with my life so that it will not turn out to be a lost cause. Amen.

I thought of Carolyn, as she became more proficient in her lock-smith job, being "called out" at night to help solve problems connected with the gates and doors of the prison. Her mechanical skills, related to the institutional objective of keeping doors locked, became an instrument of God's gift of deliverance in her life. I was reminded of a story in the book of Acts about prison gates being opened in the night. Some of the apostles, the lesson tells us, were arrested in Jerusalem for exercising their ministry in Christ's name and were put in prison.

> *But at night an angel of the Lord opened the prison doors*
> *and brought them out and said,*
> *'Go and stand in the temple and speak to the people*
> *all the words of this Life.'*
>
> —Acts 5:19–20

Singing, as a form of spiritual deliverance, has special meaning for those who live with the thought that they may never be released from prison. The strength for living it imparts has little to do with being resigned to one's fate or to living with false hope. Instead, it has to do with the joy of knowing the One who sets the captives free. Lee Griffith writes:

> The miraculous nature of the apostles' deliverance from prison in Acts can be understood in the light of the identification of prisons with the power of death and the identification of Jesus as one who frees the prisoners.[6]

God is fittingly praised with a song of freedom whenever the weight of prison upon human lives is lifted. The Master Singer calls us to be a part of a prayerful movement on behalf of those who long to be free from the power of the prison to defeat the human spirit. This, in turn, allows the prisoners themselves to become actors and musicians in a modern day drama of pre-release deliverance.

> O master singer, teach me now, teach me to sing in every part; a song to open prison doors, to set all souls and spirits free, a song whose hearing changes time and brings the year of jubilee. Sing, sing![7]

---

6. Griffith, *The Fall of the Prison*, 115.

7. Words from the hymn, "If I Could Teach," written by Ken Medema. Used by permission of Briar Patch Music/Ken Medema Music. Copyright © 2005, Ken Medema Music.

10

Returning, Resting and Remembering

And the ransomed of the Lord shall return, and come to Zion
with singing; everlasting joy shall be upon their heads;
they shall obtain joy and gladness and sorrow and sighing will flee away.

—Isaiah 35:10

THE BABYLONIAN CAPTIVES, FREE at last to return to their homeland, were filled with joy over the thought of returning home. The first ones to appear at the gates of Jerusalem were strangers to the people who were living there. As the returning exiles entered the city, it is not difficult to imagine how those who greeted them wondered how much of Babylon they were bringing home with them. No one could fully grasp what the years of captivity had done to them or if they would ever be complacent enough again to feel "at ease in Zion" (Amos 6:1), their spiritual home.

When King Artaxerexes sent Nehemiah to rebuild the walls of Jerusalem, the work was completed before all of the exiles had returned home from Babylon. Later, Ezra, the priest and scribe who was closely associated with Nehemiah during the construction years, delivered a long sermon to a crowd that included many of the former captives. He first reminded them of how many times they had been disobedient to God and had suffered as a result. But then, with emphasis and sincerity, he uttered the word, "nevertheless." In spite of their waywardness and in spite of the pain of separation it caused, God's emphatic *nevertheless* rang joyously in their ears as songs of celebration over the re-building of their nation were sung.

Nevertheless, in your great mercies you did not make an end of them or
forsake them, for you are a gracious and merciful God.

—Nehemiah 9:31

RETURNING

There are men and women today who, upon their release from prison, are fortunate to have family members who will welcome them home. Many weep tears of joy over their acceptance and for the help they are given in re-building their lives. On the other hand, there are many newly released offenders who have no one to rejoice with them over their release. They are quickly identified when they step off the bus by the small bag of personal belongings they carry. The majority of them want to be self-supporting, but work is hard to find and they only have a few dollars in their pockets. They fully expect, when they check the "box" on job applications that reveals their prison background, that they will be immediately eliminated from consideration. Some of them, as a result, end up at the mercy of people who have set up shop on the streets of futility and who are bent on claiming those upon whose faces the marks of prison are clearly evident. These shadowy figures lurk about familiar release locations waiting for an "easy mark" to make their day.

The number of released offenders who will end up back in prison is commonly estimated to be as high as sixty-five percent. Regularly quoted statistics also reveal the sad fact that more than half of those who get out of prison will return within three years. A *Christian Science Monitor* article by Kris Axtman quotes Mario Paparozzi, a justice expert at the College of New Jersey and former chairman of the New Jersey Parole Board:

> The reentry issue must be dealt with while a person is still incarcerated. Successful reentry creates a thoughtful review and release process and rethinking how best to use already available resources. It means building strong ties between local housing authorities, police and businesses. In short it means owning crime as a social problem.[1]

Many of those who return from prison to the so-called free world find it difficult to become self-supportive. To really become free requires avoiding the lure of illicit gain and the borderline pleasures that result, at times, in unexpected trouble. A resolution, important to meeting these challenges, is found in the hymn written by Edwin Mote, "My Hope is Built." It is: "I dare not trust the sweetest frame, but wholly lean on Jesus' Name."

---

1. Axtman, "A Flood of Parolees Hits the Streets," lines 51–57. Reprinted with permission from *The Christian Science Monitor*. All rights reserved.

There is general agreement among those who have recently returned home from prison that what they imagined about how life would be for them outside of prison was far from being realistic. As a result, their adjustment to life outside of prison takes longer than they anticipated and the feeling they have of carrying a sign that tells everyone where they have been is not easily dispelled. Where they once gave little thought to how they would get to parole appointments, they suddenly face the problem of transportation. Where they once felt confident about being able to find a job, they abruptly face rejection, and where in prison they received no bill for a doctor's visit, now the problem is the payment. Other considerations unimagined in prison, such as learning how to balance a free-world diet, setting the internal clock for sleeping, and mentally absorbing how much things have changed, are suddenly items of daily concern in the "world."

Jorge Antonio Renaud, from whom I obtained permission to quote from his work, was paroled on July 2, 2008, after serving nearly 17 years in Texas prisons. An article he wrote for the 2008 Summer edition of the *TIFA Contact* presents an excellent summation of what it takes to make it in the world outside of prison. His repeated refrain is, "I asked, I learned, I adjusted."[2]

There are some family members who, in welcoming loved ones home, end up contributing to the problems of their adjustment. Their vigilance may be over extended. They may offer too much too soon or be too fearful in advising against what they believe to be excesses. They may be too slow in allowing the home-from-prison loved one to move into a responsible and comfortable routine. There may be older children who find it hard to accept a long absent parent's expectation of being able to resume a position of authority over them. No matter how hard a loving family may try, there are no guarantees of freedom from temptation and trouble.

As love prevails and responsibilities are shared, a loved one's coming home from prison can be celebrated as the fulfillment of many days of preparation. A mother, joyous over a daughter's return, prepares a variety of delicious meals. Chocolate chip cookies disappear as soon as they come out of the oven. The family worships together in church, conversations are spiced with laughter, and good cheer accompanies the breaking of each new day. The shared responsibility of helping to shape a future of honor and blessing is taken up within a family circle of prayer and praise.

2. Readers may request of a copy of the article, "You're Adjusting So Well," by emailing tifa@tifa.org.

RESTING

For thus said the Lord God, the Holy One of Israel:
In returning and rest you shall be saved;
in quietness and in trust shall be your strength.

—Isaiah 30:15

The necessary amount of rest is often hard to obtain for those who return to their homes after being released from prison. They should be encouraged to take advantage of rest periods available to them especially as they feel the urgent need to get busy, to pay back, and—at last—to know they really belong. The need they have to slowly breathe in the air of freedom increases the importance of having people around them who love them and who can help them form habits that include the blessing of rest.

Men and women who took time in prison for prayer and the study of scripture may find, after they are released, that their devotional life is less concentrated. Overwhelmed by the number of things to be done that include the strain of personal decision-making and job interviews, they may find themselves becoming tired and irritable. Those who have thought so long about what they were missing on the outside need the kind of rest that calms their obsessive desire to make up for the lost years and that replenishes the body, mind, and spirit for living in God's peace through each day.

The confidence needed by newly released offenders in meeting people and making personal decisions is not easily obtained because of the negative connotations associated with having been in prison. At the close of each day, it helps to say, in the way of the psalmist:

Return, O my soul, to your rest,
for the Lord has dealt bountifully with you.

—Psalm 116:7

REMEMBERING

Remember those who are in prison,
as though you were in prison with them.

—Hebrews 13:3

To remember those in prison, even in a general sort of way, is not an easy requirement to fulfill. While we remember special events in our lives, as well as people who are important to us, Jesus calls us to remember prisoners. If we pass them by, it is like passing him by. If we choose to visit a prisoner in Jesus' name, or even pray for a prisoner, we may be healed of our impulse to isolate ourselves from those whose future could depend upon whether or not they are so remembered.

Our disciplined remembrance of those in prison will make a difference in our lives as well as theirs. Examples of this are found within a service-oriented kind of remembering such as collecting and delivering toiletry items for indigent offenders, becoming involved in group ministries to prisoners, teaching a Bible study class, or becoming a mentor or pen pal. Such remembering allows us to live expectantly, celebrating the good news of the kingdom as if the prison gates had already opened.

Christian remembering includes men and women who are recognized as victims and who are both sad and angry over the thought that someone is serving too little time in prison rather than too much. Sometimes, our active remembering of those who have suffered from having a criminal act committed against them will prompt us to pray for them. Or, we may be able to offer them comfort and peace through a song such as the one that tells of "a place of quiet rest, near to the heart of God."[3]

Those who visit a loved one in prison become aware that the treatment of prisoners by correctional officers does not include much kindness. However, family members should not allow that fact to keep them from courteously presenting themselves to everyone they meet who works for the prison. When that condition is fulfilled, there will be evidence from time to time of how much better kind words are than angry words. A good example of how this can be is found in the story of Joseph who, while in prison, earned the respect of the chief of the Pharoah's jail.

3. From "Near to the Heart of God," written by Cleland B. McAfee.

The chief jailer committed to Joseph's care all the prisoners who were in the prison, and whatever was done there, he was the one who did it. The chief jailer gave no heed to anything that was in Joseph's care, because the Lord was with him; and whatever he did, the Lord made it prosper.

—Genesis 39:22–23

Those who have been released from prison will retain memories of how it was for them when they were inside the controlled compound. The tortuous days and nights will not be forgotten. Their remembering may occur in unpleasant dreams or through sobering reminders of what their loved ones went through at home while they were away. Some will remain faithful to the hope that fueled their desire for release. Others will seek to forget by locating themselves as far away as possible from any reminders of the past. There is no way, of course, to undo what happened that resulted in having to serve time in prison, but there is a way to receive, joyously and thankfully, opportunities for a new life after prison time is over. These opportunities take root in minds and hearts that continue to remain free from the type of negative influences that once pulled them down.

For those whose lives seem broken beyond repair, remembrance may be no more than a wistful desire to be back where they do not have to be concerned about having a place to sleep, food to eat, and clothes to wear. They may think of being back among those who are like they are and who have no incentive to change, back within the familiar confines of prison. These persons, unloved and alone against the world, are among those for whom Jesus weeps.

Marilyn and I will remember our every other weekend visits with Carolyn. We will remember how her brother, Van, patiently and with great concern for his sister, took his turn so that every weekend she had a visit. We will remember how much the Kairos volunteers and the Catholic deacon helped to nourish Carolyn's faith, and we will remember how many people, in so many places, prayed for her. We will remember the officers and staff of the William P. Hobby Unit who offered their kindness to us with encouraging words about her. Finally, we will remember with thanksgiving a United Methodist minister by the name of Gary Whitbeck who month by month helped Carolyn to understand that she was accepted and forgiven.

A box at our house holds cards and letters we received from Carolyn. We save them as remembrances of her time in prison. I still keep a birthday card from Carolyn on a shelf where I can see it every day. On the outside of it there is a picture of Noah's Ark gliding across the water. The picture shows animals of all kinds aboard the vessel. Some have their heads sticking out of portholes on the side. Behind the ark, dark clouds still cast their menacing shadows, while up ahead clear skies are seen and the sun appears above the breaking clouds. Inside, she wrote the words:

> The ark is sailing out of danger—it is leaving the stormy skies be-
> hind and moving toward the rainbow which awaits its arrival into
> calmer seas. On my journey home, which of course is not quite
> complete, I feel that I am emerging from the stormy skies. This is
> a childish thing to say—but during the darkest, scariest storms—
> your strength and your faith brought me through—and so in every
> sense of the word, you are truly my hero. All my love, Carolyn.

11

Questions of Faith

When those who keep us in prison ask of us mirth
in our hang-ups with 'Sing us a song of Zion,'
what can we sing under the mourning willows
of common suffering in the river-meadows of Babel?[1]

WHEN THE CAPTIVES IN Babylon found their voices and were able to sing with confidence the songs of their faith, they were better able to live with the indignities of their subservient status. And yet, when they were first taunted by their captors and asked to sing a song of Zion, the question they asked was, "What can we sing?"

WHAT CAN WE SING?

The gift of being able to sing through the trials and tribulations of being locked up in prison dramatizes the truth that opens the gates to freedom. Singing contributes to the patience of being still, even as it fuels the impatience required to move forward. In the stillness, as well as in the restlessness, we know that God cares for those who, in so many ways, prison diminishes. The same holds true for the loved ones of prisoners. The life-giving element of an endless song is realized through the descriptive notes of a nineteenth-century hymn:

> Through all the tumult and the strife
> I hear that music ringing.
> It finds an echo in my soul.
> How can I keep from singing?[2]

1. Davie, *To Scorch Or To Freeze*, 56.
2. From the hymn, "How Can I Keep From Singing," written by American Baptist minister Robert Lowery.

Family members, like their loved ones in prison, who excuse themselves from singing on the grounds of not being able to "carry a tune," may nonetheless be embraced by the sounds of music that carry praise and thanksgiving. Beautiful melodies convey feelings and thoughts that words cannot express. They can help to ease the trouble and sorrow of having a loved one who is in serious trouble. They can answer the daily challenge of a long journey through prison time and they can give appropriate voice to a celebration of release.

Our choice of what to sing was once determined by practices of faith far removed from the crisis of loneliness we experienced as the result of waking up in a strange land. Then, through the changed circumstances of our lives, I thought of hymns already familiar to me that offered answers to every form of trouble that might disturb our lives. One such hymn was Charles Wesley's, "Thou Hidden Source of Calm Repose."

In want my plentiful supply, in weakness my almighty power, In bonds my perfect liberty, my light in Satan's darkest hour, In grief my joy unspeakable, my life in death, my heaven in hell.

—fourth stanza

Prayers to God on our behalf enabled us to recover our voices "under the mourning willows of a common suffering."[3] We went forward with relief over how well Carolyn was managing her time in prison and our songs became thankful offerings to God for bringing all of us "through the deep waters."[4]

Given my love of traditional hymns of Christian worship, I would have thought it impossible to be impressed favorably by rap music. So, I was surprised when I heard three young men perform and was moved by their performance as well as the reception it received from the large audience. They were participants in a substance abuse treatment program located in a facility near Humble, Texas. Marilyn and I attended a graduation ceremony that day in support of a young man I had visited in the Harris County Jail. We were impressed with the program, the staff *and* the rap music. The snap and pop of the rhythmic beat, accompanied by words about "hurting mother" and "regrets," gave the audience of program mem-

3. Davie, *To Scorch Or To Freeze*, 56.
4. Hymn, "How Firm a Foundation," "K" in Rippon's *A Selection of Hymns*, 1787.

bers in earlier phases of training, as well as family members, something to vigorously applaud. These young men have discovered through their music that the place where they are staying is not so strange when the love they share is genuine. Words applicable to healing possibilities and set to a fast-paced beat are apparently helpful in opening the lives of young offenders to a better future. The fact that they were shouted out with such seriousness gave their testimony of remorse and their expressions of joy a touching authenticity.

Music preferred by a younger generation can be therapeutic in introducing them to the sobriety appropriate to a new life. When employed in conjunction with caring ways of instruction and discipline, such music may help to bring about positive changes. These nontraditional forms of musical expression, while keeping thoughts of pain and remorse within the lyrics, help to reduce the trouble-options available to young people who are particularly vulnerable. They signal how important it is that "our praise should be shaped by cruciform joy, music capable of embracing our deepest fears and our highest hopes, our most intense griefs as well as our most focused triumphs."[5]

Inspired by singing the Lord's songs in a strange land, Marilyn and I have learned how to assist those who visit loved ones in prison. Our conversations with strangers who are experiencing the difficulties of prison visitation play out in different ways. The idea of "performing the gospel," as explained by Stanley Hauerwas, reminds me of how our ministry is musically scripted.

> What it means to be a good performer of the gospel, then, is not simply a matter of finding the right words—although it is clearly that—but it is also a matter of finding the right key in which to sing our song, the right meter and cadence in which to say our poem, the right register in which to play our piece.[6]

As we moved through the years of Carolyn's incarceration at the William P. Hobby Unit, I thought about what songs might come to her as she waited for the time of her prison confinement to end. I wondered if she remembered a song called "It's A New Found Joy" that she learned as a young girl in Sunday School. Or, if she remembered the melodious "Hymn of Promise" from the time she listened to her mother playing it

5. S. Jones and L. G. Jones, "Worship, the Eucharist, Baptism and Aging," 195.
6. Hauerwas, *Performing the Faith*, 102.

on the piano during one of the collect telephone calls she made from the
Harris County Jail.

> *There's a song in every silence, seeking word and melody;*
> *there's a dawn in every darkness, bringing hope to you and me.*
> *From the past will come the future; what it holds a mystery,*
> *unrevealed until its season, something God alone can see.*[7]

—Natalie Sleeth

HOW CAN WE SERVE?

> *To serve the present age, my calling to fulfill;*
> *O may it all my powers engage to do my Master's will!*

—Charles Wesley

When our powers are engaged to carry gifts of love and mercy to
those in prison, it often happens as the result of being influenced by a
tragedy of one kind or another. As Stanley Hauerwas suggests,

> The church is thus those whose lives have been opened by God,
> often an opening that has been extracted at great cost, and so
> are capable of being open to others without fear or resentment.
> Hospitality is part of their holiness, as they have learned to wel-
> come the stranger as the very presence of God.[8]

Henry Covert, in the introduction to his book, *Ministry to the
Incarcerated,* writes about what it takes for anyone to make such a faith
commitment.

> . . . taking up the cross means a death to self-serving will and an
> acceptance of the responsibility and pain that accompanies iden-
> tification and involvement with the oppressed. We must move
> beyond rhetoric and concern to concrete forms of action.[9]

7. From "Hymn of Promise," written by Natalie Sleeth. Copyright© 1986 Hope
Publishing Company, Carol Stream, IL 60188. All rights reserved. Used by permission.

8. Hauerwas, *The Peaceable Kingdom,* 146.

9. Covert, *Ministry to the Incarcerated,* xii.

As an outcome of understanding what God had made possible in our lives, I accepted an invitation, at the beginning of our earliest experiences with county jails, to help organize a prison ministry program through St. Luke's United Methodist Church. We called it the Newgate Connection after the prison in London where the early Methodists, led by John and Charles Wesley, regularly preached to the prisoners. Marilyn and I started by learning as much as possible about existing ministries. I had already been introduced to Prison Fellowship's InnerChange Freedom Initiative (IFI) located within what is now the Carol Vance Unit at Richmond, Texas. During that time I visited with offenders who were having special problems, celebrated the Sacrament of the Lord's Supper with the IFI class, and visited in their dorm.

Prison Fellowship's Angel Tree was one of the first programs that attracted our interest. We became involved, near Christmas, in providing gifts for children with a father or mother in prison. Later, we collected books for prison libraries and assisted a group of volunteers who, under the dynamic leadership of a lady named Rebecca Howard, handed out pairs of warm socks to county jail inmates.

The two ministers, Ron Morris and Terry Thompson, who visited Carolyn in the Harris County Jail, knew us well enough to know that we might be willing to help those with whom they came in contact who had family members in jail. The first call I received sent me to the Harris County Jail to visit a young man charged with a drug-related offense. Marilyn and I talked to his mother over the telephone and, soon thereafter, we met his mother and father at a local chapter meeting of the Texas Inmate Families Association. As time passed, I received other calls from parents asking for help. After my jail visits, Marilyn often joined me in talking in person or on the telephone with the parents. She shared helpful information with them, identifying in a special way with mothers.

Offenders who I visit are sincere in their expressions of gratitude. It is easy to assume, as I did at first, that they will never return to jail or prison. I learned to my disappointment, however, that not everyone who listens to words of encouragement and hope will become free enough to ward off the temptations that trigger repeat offenses. Some offenders are so tragically conditioned by drug-related habits that they find it hard, no matter how much they are prayed over and coached, to work their way out of such attachments. Many live within the middle ground of trying to establish a better life while continuing to be drawn to people who have surrendered their lives to the drug culture.

The majority of the men and women I have visited in jails and prisons leave no trail behind them when they get out and I do not expect to hear from them again. On the other hand, we have had some rewarding experiences following an offender's prison time. One such instance took place when Marilyn and I picked up a man being released from a state jail and I subsequently officiated at the marriage ceremony that re-united him with his former wife. Another man who vowed he would never go back to jail gave me a handwritten copy of his personal journal with a note attached that read: "In case you ever meet someone who you think might benefit from reading the story of my life."

In 1998, the Administrator of Chaplain Services for the state, Jerry Groom, suggested to us that we might like to begin a hospitality ministry to those who visited loved ones at the L. G. Plane State Jail. Marilyn and I accepted the challenge and returned as volunteers to the broad walk leading into the front door of the same jail where we had visited Carolyn. Warden June Groom offered to supply a water cooler, which was placed just outside the door, and Chaplain Glory Siller was available to us on the opening day. We began our ministry by offering a cup of cold water to the people who stood in line during the July heat.

Marilyn and I were soon loaning items of clothing, donated by churches, to the men and women who arrived not dressed according to the prison system's guidelines. We shared information with the visitors about matters related to their loved ones and helped those who were visiting for the first time to understand what would happen when they walked through the front doors. Frequently, we were asked the question, "Why are you doing this?" We replied, "Because we have stood where you are standing."

Anne Holloman, during the earliest days of our volunteer work at the L. G. Plane State Jail for Women, distinguished herself through a valuable ministry to children who were brought by relatives to visit their mothers. At the time, she was on the Outreach Ministries Staff of St. Luke's United Methodist Church. Armed with a fresh supply of children's books, Anne set up a Saturday schedule of reading to the children. A prison owned rocking chair, by way of Anne's insistence, was placed in a visitation area alcove on a rug donated by St. Luke's. When the children grew restless while sitting at a visitation table or being held by their mothers, Anne invited them over to the reading area. We would see her occasionally, when we entered the building, with a young child in her lap while older children sat on the rug, all of them listening to her read the stories.

Not long afterward, during the time we were assisting the visitors who waited in line, Jerry Groom casually suggested to us that a building designed for the comfort and assistance of visitors would be a great blessing. Such a building, he emphasized, would help a much larger number of visitors. First, it would serve the needs of all three of the Dayton prisons. Second, it would help many more visitors since it would be open from morning until evening on both Saturday and Sunday. His idea started our thinking about how such a facility might be built.

St. Luke's United Methodist Church was the place where a contact was made that put the idea of building a Family Visitors' Center, a name suggested by Jerry Groom, into the realm of possibility. The breakthrough came after the women's choir of the Plane State Jail sang at a morning worship service at St. Luke's. Their songs touched the hearts of many in the congregation including Jack Blanton who, at the time, was President of Houston Endowment, an organization devoted to the financial support of worthy projects in the Houston area. After receiving an initial grant of $200,000 from Houston Endowment, Inc., the total of $300,000 was reached through smaller gifts from many different sources. The vision of what this service of welcome and relief would mean to the family members of prisoners caught the attention of area churches and groups engaged in prison ministry.

The dedication ceremony for the Family Visitors' Center took place on September 11, 2001. The crowd, many of whom had just heard of the tragic destruction of the twin towers in New York City, listened to the women's choir from the Plane State Jail sing about the Holy Spirit coming down. Officials from the Texas Department of Criminal Justice were present along with representatives from each of the three prisons. The Mission Director of The Trinity River Baptist Association and members of Chapels of Hope, Dayton Complex, the organization that managed the details of building construction and served as the fiscal intermediary, were there. Pastors and members of churches were in attendance along with our special friends from St. Luke's United Methodist Church and St. Paul's United Methodist Church. The Assistant Warden of the L. V. Hightower Unit presided over the event as chaplains of each of the three state prison facilities took part in the ceremony.

The Family Visitors' Center opened to receive visitors on December 22, 2001. The six volunteers who were present greeted 282 visitors who came for Christmas visits with loved ones in prison. Over 12,000 visitors came through this building, located on prison ground, during the period from October 1, 2004 through September 30, 2005. During that same time, 602 items of clothing were loaned to visitors. Fifty-two volunteers representing sixteen different churches, many of them a part of the Trinity River Baptist Association, were involved in keeping the building open each weekend. The lesson we used to describe this hospitality ministry is found in the Bible's book of Hebrews:

> *Be not forgetful to entertain strangers,*
> *for thereby some have entertained angels unawares.*

—Hebrews 13:2–3a (KJV)

Marilyn and I drove to Austin, Texas, on May 23, 2007, to present a program at the Travis County State Jail about our Family Visitors' Center ministry. Joan Burnham, former Executive Director of the Texas Inmate Families Association, asked me if we would be willing to come to Austin and offer them some operational advice related to a visitation center they were planning to build adjacent to the Travis County State Jail.

Representatives of the sponsoring organizations,[10] ministry groups, and service agencies were present for the program, which was held in the contact visitation room. In addition, several TDCJ officials were there along with a number of the staff of the Travis County State Jail. Marilyn and I appreciated the obvious concern of the participants for the cause with which we have been identified through church and community. On that unusual day, the prison became a place of spirited conversation about welcome, advocacy, and restoration. Before we left, I was surprised when a captain who works visitation at the facility thanked me for my explanation of what family members often experience when they come for visits.

Marilyn and I have found special fulfillment through our service to family members and friends of prisoners, as well as to prisoners themselves. This work was begun while Carolyn was still in prison and has

---

10. Sponsoring organizations include The Austin/Travis County Reentry Roundtable, Criminal Justice Planning (Travis County), and Criminal Justice Center (CJC) Advisory Committee.

continued following her release. We have been greatly blessed by entering places where being divested of all that represents worldly power is a requirement of admission. This movement of faith, I believe, is fulfilled by accepting the terms of discipleship as they derive from the love of God. I give thanks that we have been granted so many ways to see how, against the forces of unprincipled power, the weakness of the crucified savior is able to become the strength of love's redeeming work, a work that enables goodness and mercy to reach into the depths of human need. As Jean Vanier has written:

> Yes, through our wounds the power of God can penetrate us and become like rivers of living water to irrigate the arid earth within us. Thus we may irrigate the arid earth of others, so that hope and love are reborn.[11]

11. Vanier, *The Broken Body*, 61.

12

Homecoming

I believe that home is Christ's kingdom which exists both within us and
among us as we wend our prodigal way through the world in search of it.[1]

—Frederick Buechner

MARILYN RECEIVED A TELEPHONE call from Gary Whitbeck on an afternoon when I was away from the house. He had just completed his visit with Carolyn and was calling from the parking lot of the William P. Hobby Unit. He told her that Carolyn had received word of the decision of the Texas Board of Pardons and Paroles to release her from prison on parole. When Marilyn called me, she was crying for joy as I heard her say, through her tears, that Carolyn was coming home.

Our next visit with Carolyn, following the wonderful news about her release approval, was as joyous as any prison visit can be. She told us that many of the officers had found out and were extending special congratulations to her.

In thinking back on what took place before the news of Carolyn's release came to us, I remember our second trip to Gatesville to make our case for her parole. Vic Driscoll, an attorney friend of Bill Burge, who was giving us some assistance in preparing for Carolyn's review, went with us. Vic thoughtfully presented the key points of Carolyn's request for release on parole to the same board member who reviewed Carolyn's case with us three years before. Marilyn and I felt free to inject comments related to Carolyn's health problems and were encouraged by his interest in what we told him. He said that he would try to visit her at the Hobby Unit the next day. Finally, we were happily surprised when he said that he would like to talk with Gary Whitbeck. I promised to get Gary's telephone number to

1. Buechner, *The Longing for Home*, 28.

him the next morning. We left the parole board office with the assurance that everything possible had been done.

Marilyn and I, on our last visit with Carolyn at the Hobby Unit, felt as if the two hours passed more quickly than ever before. As we walked out of the building, got into our car, and drove away from the place where we had spent so many hours, we were relieved by the thought that Carolyn's prison time was winding down.

As Marilyn and I tried to imagine what it would be like to have Carolyn with us, we kept returning in our hearts to the songs we had learned for a strange land. We remembered how, at certain times, they helped to penetrate the gloom of a dark night and provided us with direction through days of sadness and uncertainty. Now, we would be singing many of the same familiar hymns of faith with a wonderful sense of expectancy as we continued to feel what we described to each other as an incredible lightness of being.

We heard, at the beginning, that Carolyn would be released within 45 days. A few days later, we were told that it would be within 60 days. When I started calling about a release date, it dawned on us again how easy it is for irrational thought to take charge. What seems like nothing more than a total lack of concern is, in reality, a careful process of investigation and computer entries designed, once again, to insure public safety.

We learned that the files of those who have been approved for release circulate from one address to another, sometimes delayed by holidays. But after almost two months had passed without having received a release date, we became more and more anxious. We started guessing when our last trip to the prison would take place and if it would be the two of us or Van who would have the honor. On one visit we brought home some of Carolyn's "property" so that her load would be lighter when they took her to Gatesville for her release.

One of our greatest concerns during those days of waiting was the pain we knew Carolyn was suffering as the result of arthritis. She mentioned to us on one of our visits that the authorities at the William P. Hobby Unit had instituted a "standing count" at 2:00 a.m. each morning. The pain made it hard for Carolyn to get out of bed. She said that she slept a schedule that enabled her to wake up before the count in order to prepare herself for standing. Within a sadness that was eased only by the excitement of her impending release, we prayed that God would give her the strength she needed to get through each day aided, in a number of ways, by inmate friends. Marilyn and I were sustained by thoughts of how wonderful it would be to experience the long-awaited fulfillment of what I once described as "calling Carolyn home."

After making many telephone calls, we finally learned that Carolyn's release date would be Tuesday, February 10, 2004. We notified Gary Whitbeck and he expressed confidence that he and his wife, Paula, would be there with us. Emmett Solomon provided us with information that First United Methodist Church in Gatesville was involved in the First Contact ministry that provides volunteers who are permitted into the unit to meet with the women who are getting out the next day. I called the pastor, Johnny Miller, who told me that he would go early on the morning of Carolyn's release to visit with her and the others who were being released.

Marilyn and I spent the night in Gatesville in order to be rested for the great event. At 9:30 the next morning, we met Gary and Paula and drove to the Gatesville Unit, where women due for release make their exit from prison. There, we were told that it would be 11:00 a.m. before anyone could be picked up. So, we went back to the church, returning a few minutes before the designated hour. We were instructed to remain in the car as we drove up to the gate that represented for Carolyn the final step into a world from which she had been separated for eight and one-half years. Only one other family was present to pick up their loved one. The six others being released that morning were to be put on a bus for a trip to their drop-off locations, a sad reminder of how many do not have anyone to meet them at the gate.

We will never forget the sight of Carolyn coming down the walk of the Gatesville Release Center. She was carrying an orange mesh bag that held her prison possessions and was dressed in the hospital scrubs that are often supplied as release clothing by the prisons. We watched as a female officer accompanied Carolyn and one other woman who was being released to family members. After Carolyn passed through the prison gate and got into the car, we greeted her quietly.

Gary and Paula Whitbeck were special to us in those moments when Carolyn walked free of the restrictive custody of the Texas Department of Criminal Justice. Their being with us was a blessing of friendship we will always remember.

Johnny Miller met us back at the church where we took pictures, Carolyn changed into the clothes her mother had brought, and more pictures were taken. The six of us held hands in a tight circle and Johnny prayed. After saying one last "thank you" to our friends, the three of us, Marilyn, Carolyn, and I, waved good-bye to them and started home. From Temple, Texas, all the way to Houston, it rained unceasingly but our joy was not one bit dampened. We got home before the shades of a cloudy evening became night and, upon our arrival, gave thanks to God.

PRAISE THE LORD!

Sing to the Lord a new song,
his praise in the assembly of the faithful.

—Psalm 149:1

When Carolyn returned home from prison, Marilyn and I started talking about having a service of thanksgiving to God for her deliverance. We remembered Gary's letter, following the disappointment of her three-year set-off by the parole board, encouraging us to "look forward to the grand celebration we will have when she is released."

On the afternoon of March 29, 2004 an "assembly of the faithful" gathered in the chapel of Holly Hall for a homecoming service for Carolyn. Residents, many of whom had prayed for all of us through the years, were present in the congregation. Susan Kern, one of Carolyn's longtime friends, joined Van in walking her down the aisle to begin the service. Gary Whitbeck, whose availability was determined before anything else in planning the service, came from Georgetown to bring the message. Marilyn played the organ. Her music included, at a special point, the "Hymn of Promise." I conducted the service and Van set up a recorder in order to preserve the words and music of such an amazing experience of praise and thanksgiving.

Gary's message included special thoughts about Carolyn and how the promise of God's guidance was always present through his years of visiting her. He concluded by asking Carolyn if she would like to speak. She responded by expressing her thanks to everyone for the prayers and support that she and her family had received. Then, all the ministers and chaplains in attendance were invited to come forward and place their hands on Carolyn as Gary Whitbeck asked God's blessing upon her. Our friend, Bishop Ben Oliphint who, along with his wife Nancy, had supported us through special gifts of love and kindness, gave the benediction.

The people were invited to the activities building where each one was able to meet Carolyn and where I was able to make some introductions.

The prayers Marilyn and I said over and over during the years of Carolyn's prison time prepared us for her homecoming. In thankfulness to God, we joyfully celebrated the victory represented by her release. As the four of us sat down at our table for a meal that Marilyn prepared, we talked together in the special ways that hold a family together. The fulfillment of our work and prayer is appropriately expressed in the words of the hymn:

In faith we'll gather round the table to taste and share what love can do. This is a day of new beginnings; our God is making all things new.[2]

—Brian Wren

FINDING THE WAY

Carolyn reached beyond herself in living and working inside the prison while, at the same time, being aware of what it was about prison that caused her to long for freedom. When she came home and reached within herself for the kind of helpful assistance she had for so many years thought about providing for us, she came up disappointed. She was physically unable to perform the jobs around the house that she wanted to do immediately after she came home.

Carolyn's first months of freedom were spent wearing an ankle monitor as a condition of her parole. She was required to take a class and to report to the parole office on a regular schedule. Other things that took time to accomplish included obtaining a driver's license, learning how to use the computer, and scheduling job interviews. Through one rejection after another, she exhibited no signs of anger or resentment, only occasional frustration over the time it took to regain her strength. While she learned to live with the quiet of the night, she could not accept the unfamiliar darkness for sleeping.

The first time we worshipped together at St. Luke's, our pastor, Jim Moore, greeted us warmly and extended his arms of welcome to Carolyn.

2. From the hymn, "This is a Day of New Beginnings," written by Brian Wren. Copyright © 1986 Hope Publishing Company, Carol Stream, IL 60188. Used by permission. All rights reserved.

A few weeks later, we rejoiced that Carolyn was given an opportunity to contribute, through her skilled use of the Spanish language, to a St. Luke's outreach ministry, the Jingle Bell Express, that made clothing and other necessities available to those in need.

While Carolyn was busy setting up job interviews, she worked several part-time jobs, the most important one being house repair work for her uncle, Bill Andel. Later, Carolyn was recommended for a job with a well established nonprofit corporation by a special representative of TDCJ's Project RIO (Re-Integration of Offenders). After being interviewed by the Executive Director of that organization, Carolyn was hired. She was grateful for the opportunity to prove her competency and reliability in the kind of faith-centered work that provides an important service for those with limited financial resources.

On August 5, 2006, Carolyn boarded an Intercontinental Airlines flight to Honduras with twelve volunteers who were going to Santa Rosa de Copan, Honduras, to assist with a special project. She helped with the work but, with her language skills, she also served a valuable function as the interpreter. She called us that evening to let us know they had arrived safely. During her second call, on Monday, she told us about attending a church service on Sunday evening. She said she had heard the bells from a church near the hotel calling the people to worship and decided, with one of the volunteers, to attend. She told us how a large crowd of people, the majority standing, heard the priest say at the beginning of the service, "Let us remember that we have nothing." Later that week, she and another volunteer visited the prison in Santa Rosa de Copan and, while there, purchased several beautiful hammocks made by the prisoners. She will remember Honduras and will cherish the memory of the children calling to her in the Spanish translation of her name, "Carolina! Carolina!"

Thanks be to God! Carolyn is at home in a way that astounds us with its grace and favor. Abiding in the love of God, we have everything.

Acknowledgments

MY SON, VAN, AN Academic Adviser at the University of Houston, read through multiple drafts of the slowly developing manuscript and raised important questions related to language and meaning. His notes in the margins gave me clues that led to some important revisions. Van's review of the almost completed project included some encouraging words that kept me on the track to completion.

I am fortunate to have had Nancy Shoptaw as copyeditor of this project. She brought skill and patience to the important task of fulfilling the publisher's guidelines while remaining sensitive to the story we continue to live as a family.

I have been blessed by the consideration of four men whose careers combine a broad range of academic achievement and faithfulness to the church. The work of each one includes the writing of excellent books. Paul Jones, Richard Morgan, Stanley Hauerwas, and Walter Brueggemann offered their friendship to me in ways unique to each one.

I met Paul Jones during my doctor of ministry studies at St. Paul School of Theology in Kansas City, Missouri, when he directed that program. Paul's life journey includes experiences as a United Methodist minister, a seminary professor, a Roman Catholic priest (Marilyn and I attended his ordination service), and a social justice activist who regularly visits prisoners located on Missouri's Death Row. His soul is nourished by the daily offices of his priestly ministry and the music of the church. I will not forget his kindness in listening to my sorrowful words at the beginning of Carolyn's time of trouble and how an important letter he wrote to Carolyn gave her a different perspective on her cell confinement.

Richard Morgan, like Paul Jones, delivered a key message during Holly Hall's ten-year lecture series focused on religion and aging. A teacher and preacher of great sensitivity to the needs of the elderly and infirm, we met after he read an article I wrote for the Journal of Religious Gerontology. His devotional writing, published by Upper Room Books, has reached a wide audience. I will always remember, as will Carolyn, the day he went with me to visit her in the Harris County Jail. Also, it was Richard Morgan who kept our names posted on the Upper Room Prayer Line.

Stanley Hauerwas, Professor of Theological Ethics at the Divinity School of Duke University, came into our lives beginning at Lake Junaluska, North Carolina, where he was leading a workshop called "Holy Living, Holy Dying." Later, I became a beneficiary of excellent reading suggestions from Hauerwas (Anthony Trollope being a notable example) and occasional drafts of papers he had written on subjects related to what he knew were my interests. I have been enriched in my life by his friendship that included, at the time of our deepest need, a letter and books he mailed to Carolyn.

Walter Brueggemann, Professor Emeritus of Old Testament at Columbia Theological Seminary at Decatur, Georgia, is a teacher, preacher, and author for whom I have great respect. His letters to me, shared with my family, lifted our spirits through Carolyn's prison years. I picked up his book, *The Message of the Psalms: A Theological Commentary*, during the earliest days of our trouble when I was looking for answers of faith for a time of unusual sadness and disorientation. The book, which is marked up and has pages coming out, will stay with me as a reminder of the psalms, their raging and weeping as well as their praising and rejoicing, and of how a wintry access to joy would have remained unknown to us except for the grief.

There are fascinating, sometimes disturbing, stories told by the prisoners I have made contact with through the years. Much of what I seek to convey about prison life comes from what they have shared with me during visits and what they have written and mailed to me. They have proven that prison does not destroy the creative impulse but may indeed help through time to bring special writing talents to life.

Philip Brasfield, through an established correspondence, has demonstrated an outstanding gift of expression and, what is more important, a spiritual consciousness of God's gifts that provide him with the kind of deliverance that many outside of prison never experience. The confidence Marilyn and I had in Philip's faith in God was strengthened by a visit we had with him at the A.D. Hughes Unit in Gatesville, Texas, on August 10, 2008.

Jorge Antonio Renaud gave me permission to use anything he had written. In addition to a few of his descriptive accounts of life in prison in his book, *Behind the Walls*, I have included in an appendix on prison poetry his excellent work entitled, "Prison Moon."

I became acquainted with David Hanna as the result of an amazing letter he wrote to St. Luke's United Methodist Church that was handed to me. Many good things came out of my decision to write to David and, subsequently, to visit him. Marilyn went with me several times and we invariably came away from our visits with the feeling that he would be special in any company. David has been released from prison. He is gainfully employed in a helping profession and has the daily blessing of those who know him best.

I include within these acknowledgments the name of Bill Burge, an attorney blessed with compassion as well as skill, who became my friend during the time he was confined to his home after being diagnosed with cancer. I will always be grateful for his careful representation of Carolyn at a time when she was not in full possession of her best judgment. My visits to the Burge home included conversation about the Family Visitors' Center that was being built to serve the three prisons located at Dayton, Texas. Bill and his wife, Dottie, always asked how this project was coming and how Carolyn was getting through her time in prison. On August 6, 2001, in the sanctuary of St. Paul's United Methodist Church, I assisted Rev. Terry Thompson in the Service of Death and Resurrection for Bill Burge. I read Psalm 46:1–7 and spoke briefly of our friendship. It is fitting that I acknowledge Bill since, without his strong legal advocacy of Carolyn, this account of prison might never have been written. In addition, his request was carried out that contributions be made to the Family Visitors' Center.

I am grateful to Victor A. Driscoll, Jr., a member of St. Paul's United Methodist Church and an attorney of wit and wisdom, for going over an earlier version of the manuscript with the knowledge of one who practices criminal law. He also offered thoughts related to the theme of "singing in a strange land" that are a part of his practice of the Christian faith. He has continued, through the years, to ask me how I was coming with the writing and we visit from time to time about matters related to parole and of particular cases with which he was involved.

Marilyn and I received the prayerful support of our minister friends and their spouses of the Texas Annual Conference of the United Methodist Church. The singing of Charles Wesley's "And Are We Yet Alive," that opens each annual conference, provided us with the assurance that we were still connected to this body of God's faithful people. Words from the second stanza of that hymn held a special meaning for us.

> What troubles have we seen, what mighty conflicts past,
> Fightings without and fears within, since we assembled last.

I am thankful for the special people of St Luke's United Methodist Church who have blessed our lives in numerous ways through these years. John and Carolyn Wildenthal, along with Anne Holloman, give their time as volunteers at the Family Visitors' Center. Susan Silvus, Director of Outreach Ministries, has been helpful over the years in keeping the church acquainted with our special ministry. Juliette Morrow, Administrative Secretary, extends countless courtesies related to my multiple ministry concerns. The Chancel Choir of St. Luke's United Methodist Church, conducted by Sid Davis, gave us songs of hope for a time of trouble and songs of joy for a time of rejoicing. Tom Pace, who became the pastor of St. Luke's following the long tenure of Jim Moore, is responsive to prisoners and to the needs they have that Christians are called to meet.

I am indebted to hymn writers and choir directors, the majority of whom now abide in the "house not made with hands, eternal in the heavens" (2 Cor 5:1b). In Christ, they represent a strength through which the church sings its faith. Together with a mother who loved poetry and hymn singing, this host of witnesses provided and continues to provide an important way for me to rejoice in a hope that does not disappoint us.

There are men and women employed by jails and prisons who, in brief moments of meeting, revealed to me how it is possible to work in places of pain without sacrificing a spirit of helpfulness. I am grateful for their unselfconscious testimonies to something far better than the prison itself represents. Otherwise, it would have been all too easy to surrender to the thought that nothing good can exist where such a burden of hopelessness is carried by so many.

Above all else, I would not have been able to continue with this drawn-out effort without the support and encouragement I receive daily from my wife, Marilyn. Her review of the completed manuscript brought about improvements in sentence structure and overall clarity. As my partner in ministry and in life, Marilyn brings laughter, light-heartedness, and music to those who know her best. While deeply conscious of the sorrows of a strange land, there is no shadow of uncertainty in her devotion to those who endure its pain. With the objective of encouragement and practical helpfulness in mind, she joins me in seeking to fulfill what the refrain of the hymn by Mary A. Thompson, "O Zion, Haste," calls us to do.

> Publish glad tidings,
> Tidings of peace;
> Tidings of Jesus,
> Redemption and release.
> Amen.

Appendix A

PRISON IN DRAMA, ART, AND ENTERTAINMENT

William Shakespeare gave the world **"King Lear."** This crowning drama reflects the tragedy of the king's blindness toward those around him and, in a sense, toward himself. At the end of the play, when about to be taken into custody with his daughter, Cordelia, Lear speaks:

> Come, let's away to prison.
> We two alone will sing like birds i' th' cage.
> When thou dost ask me blessing, I'll kneel down
> And ask of thee forgiveness. So we'll live,
> And pray, and sing, and tell old tales, and laugh
> At gilded butterflies, and hear poor rogues
> Talk of court news; and we'll talk with them too
> Who loses and who wins; who's in, who's out
> And take upon's the mystery of things,
> As if we were God's spies; and we'll wear out,
> In a wall'd prison, packs and sects of great ones
> That ebb and flow by th' moon.
>
> —King Lear V, iii, 8

Vincent Van Gogh completed a somber work entitled *The Prison Courtyard* in 1890 during his hospitalization at the Saint-Paul-de-Mausole Asylum in Saint-Remy. It was completed five months before his death from a self-inflicted gunshot wound. The painting, in which Van Gogh portrays himself, shows thirty-three inmates, temporarily released from their cells, walking grimly in a circle within a small, confining yard. The prisoners, with sloping shoulders, are watched over by three guards. They appear completely overshadowed by the high stone walls.

Johnny Cash sang to prisoners in a special way. While avoiding hard time in prison himself, Cash was able to make prisoners feel as if he knew all about their tortured lives. By writing "Folsom Prison Blues" and "San Quentin," he contributed to his reputation as an outlaw.

Sin and redemption were introduced into the music of Johnny Cash in a way that made a difference in the lives of those who listened to his prison concerts. He got away with condemning the places where they lived but did not let them off the hook for what they had done to get there. After roaring their approval of his grim stories about prison life and of drinking, robbing, and killing, he slipped them "Peace in the Valley and "He Turned the Water Into Wine."

In the movie, "**The Shawshank Redemption**," convict, Andy Dufresne, innocent of the crime of murder for which he is serving a life sentence, finds ways to cope with prison life under the leadership of a corrupt warden. Andy's cleverness eventually leads to his dramatic escape but, after one particular incident, he earns two weeks in "the hole" for a few moments during which the entire prison population stands in rapt attention to the sound of classical music.

Andy got his hands on a record that, after slipping into the control room and locking the door, he placed on a 33⅓ turntable. He turned up the sound and switched the outside speakers on. Then, he leaned back in a chair while the strains of Wolfgang Amadeus Mozart's "The Marriage of Figaro/Duettino - Sull' Aria" stunned the prisoners. To their blank world of noisy nothingness, what they heard was like a song of the angels. At the same time, one of their own was enjoying himself immensely.

Appendix B

PRISON POETRY

Spring

Ice has been cracking all day
and small boys on the shore
pretending it is the booming of artillery
lie prone clutching imaginary carbines.

Inside the compound returning birds
peck at bread scraps from the mess hall.

Old cons shiver in cloth jackets
as they cross the naked quadrangle.
They know the inside perimeter is exactly
two thousand eight-four steps
and they can walk it five more times
before a steam whistle blows for count.

Above them a tower guard dips his rifle
then raises it again dreamily.
He imagines a speckled trout
coming up shining and raging with life.[1]

—Michael Hogan

1. Hogan, "Spring," 20. Copyright © 1975 by Michael Hogan. Reprinted with permission of the author.

Appendix B

Confessions of a Jailhouse Lawyer

I grow old
Searching through dog-eared tomes
For the one case, the clincher,
Which will set me free.
In vain I search
Through the veins and arteries
Of the corpus juris,
Plumb the depths of the Pacific Reporter
In vain.
There is no such case, no such law
Because such laws were never written.

I grow musty, my spine
An old edition of Blackstone
Bent with time
My brain a collection of loose-leaf
Law Week memories.

I grow weary of helping others
To the light
At the end of the tunnel
Frightened and self-conscious in the light
Myself.

I am perhaps destined to be here
Meant to ride Rosinante through the pages
Of reported cases
And watch the bubbling lead
In the cauldron of my own absurdity.[2]

—Michael Hogan

2. Hogan, "Confessions of a Jailhouse Lawyer," 17. Copyright© 1975 by Michael Hogan. Reprinted with permission of the author.

On Looking at the Moon From Within a Prison

The first thing that comes to mind
 is distance, what's between
here and there and now and
where the whole world sleeps
which is where I do not.

The next thing that runs from my sight
are the eyes of anger, slices of white
hot, mad as hell, that carve a need in me
to make it all ok, which it will not be
anytime soon.

The best thing that comes to my mind
is looking at the moon from behind this
prison wall, begging it to come closer
as it lies on its back, sleeping or
weeping or sneaking up on the earth
poised to commit a serious crime
against darkness.

The last thing that comes to my mind
is this prison walkway, smothered
in blackness, gagged in dryness,
waiting for this moon to tilt and pour
and drench this tomb with light,
bright and cool, leaving us all dripping
and gleaming with nothing
but mercy.[3]

—Joseph Ross

3. Ross, "On Looking at the Moon From Within a Prison," 14. Used by permission of Beverly Dale, chair of the board of *The Other Side*.

23 APRIL 1977

It seems
prison confines and destroys—
it does, I know, no need to argue
the point, just look at these
infamous edifices thrashing out,
consuming
human beings like bait sardines,
but I cannot stand on this.
Yes, the great hand of prison
crushes all in its grasp,
the mind and soul become
feeble sacks
filled with rotten fruits,
a gunnysack crumpled in a dark cell.
But to control your mind and soul
is to become a stronger hand,
embanking gently the loose clods
of a ravaged and confused past
so the river of your heart
and clear streams of your soul
may pass,
full and freely, into rich fallow beds
of freedom, waiting for you
even in prison,
even in prison; many will not understand this,
but I will say that we can
overcome,
not today, tomorrow, or next month,
but at the very moment
one decides upon it.[4]

—Jimmy Santiago Baca

---

4. Baca, "23 APRIL 1977," 208–9. Used by permission of Grove/Atlantic, Inc.

Prison Moon

Four a.m. work duty and I begin
my solitary trudge from outer compound
to main building. A shivering guard,
chilled in his lonely outpost, strip searches
me until content that my inconsequential nudity
poses no threat and then whispers
the secret code that allows me admittance
into the open quarter-mile walkway.
I chuff my way into another day
as ice glints on the razor wire
and the rifles note my numbed passage,
silent but for my huffs and scuffle
on the cracked, slippery sidewalk.
A new moon, veiled in wispy fog
and beringed in glory, hangs over the prison,
its gaudy glow taunting the halogen spotlights.
The moon's creamy pull upsets
a liquid equilibrium within me
and the tides, wolves and all manner
of madmen, I surrender disturbed by the certainty that under
the bony luminescence of a grinning moon
the lunar deliriums grip me
and I howl—once, then again, and
surely somewhere an unbound sleeper stirs,
penitence is dying a giddy death.

I shake myself sane
and as the echoes hang
in the frigid air I explain
to the wide-eyed guard that convicts,
like all animals under the leash,
must bay at the beauty beyond them.[5]

—Jorge Antonio Renaud

5. First Prize Poetry from PEN American Center. Included here by permission of the author, Jorge Antonio Renaud.

Appendix C

PRISON MINISTRY ORGANIZATIONS

Bridges to Life
P.O. Box 19039
Houston, Texas 77224-9039
www.bridgestolife.org

Alpha for Prisons
P.O. Box 9359
Wichita Falls, Texas 76308
JackCowley@alphausa.org

Coalition of Prison Evangelists (COPE)
1001 W. Euless Blvd., Suite 212
Euless, TX 76040
817-684-7870
office@copeconnections.org

Camp Good News
(for children 10–15)
The Episcopal Diocese of Texas
(Camp Allen—Navasota, Texas)
Ed Davis, Coordinator
Box 398
Huntsville, Texas 77342
edsalpc@yahoo.com

Epiphany Ministry
(A Juvenile Justice Ministry)
www.epiphanyministry.org

Kairos Prison Ministry International
6907 University Boulevard
Winter Park, FL 32792
407-629-4948
nat@kairosprisonministry.org

Prison Fellowship
P.O. Box 17500
Washington, DC 20041-0500
703-904-7312
www.pfm.org

The InnerChange Freedom Initiative
Carol S. Vance Unit
2 Jester Road
Richmond, Texas 77469
281-277-8707
www.ifiprison.org

Restorative Justice Ministries Network
1229 Avenue J, Suite 360
Huntsville, Texas 77340-4629
936-291-2156
www.rjmn.net

SpritKey, Inc.
(A Re-entry Program for Ex-Offenders)
12519 Huffmeister Road
Cypress, Texas 77429
281-813-0093
allen.rice@spiritkey.org

Skills for Life: A Prison Ministry
(Toastmasters Model)
P.O. Box 38553
Houston, Texas 77238
www.skillsforlifepm.com

Appendix C

Christian Restorative Justice Mentors Association
P.O. Box 131412
The Woodlands, Texas 77393
www.crjma.org

Appendix D

CHURCH CONNECTIONS

The Baptist General Convention
Tomi Grover, Director
333 North Washington
Dallas, TX 75246-1798
214-887-5428
Tomi.Grover@bgct.org

The Catholic Church
Domestic Social Development
3211 4th Street
Washington, DC 20017-1194
202-541-3190
arivas@usccb.org

Christian Church (Disciples of Christ)
Disciples Home Missions
P.O. Box 1986
Indianapolis, IN 46206
1-888-346-2631
mail@dhm.disciples.org

The Episcopal Church, U.S.A.
Rev. Jackie Means
815 2nd Avenue
New York, NY 10017
1-800-334-7626
jmeans6482@aol.com

The Episcopal Diocese of Texas
Edwin S. Davis, Coordinator
2003 Avenue P
Huntsville, TX 77340
936-291-3153
edsalpc@yahoo.com

The Presbyterian Church (U.S.A.)
Criminal Justice Program
100 Witherspoon Street
Louisville, KY 40202-1396
502-569-5803

North American Mission Board
4200 North Point Pkwy
Alpharetta, GA 30022-4176
770-410-6000

The United Methodist Church
General Board of Global Ministries
Tanika Harris, Restorative Justice Ministries
475 Riverside Drive, Rm. 1348
New York, NY 10115
212-870-3685
tharris@gbgm-umc.org

Oklahoma Conference (United Methodist)
Criminal Justice & Mercy Ministries
Rev. Dr. Stan Basler, Director
1501 NW 24th Street
Oklahoma City, OK 73106
405-530-2015
sbasler@okumc.org

Appendix D

Texas Conference (United Methodist)
Restorative Justice Ministries
P.O. Box 131412
The Woodlands, TX 77393
281-367-3727
http://www.newgateinitiative.org

The United Church of Christ
800 Village Walk
Guilford, CT 06437-2740
1-800-653-0799

Churches of Christ Prison Ministry
Buck Griffith, Director
4420 S. Staples
Corpus Christi, TX 78411
361-992-8251

Catholic Jail and Prison Ministry
Deacon Harry Davis, Director
P.O. Box 3948
Beaumont, TX 77704-3948
409-838-0451

Appendix E

INFORMATION DIRECTORY

Advocacy and Assistance Groups
Families With Loved Ones in Prison
www.afn.org/~flip/ (with additional links)

Juvenile Justice Information Network
www.juvenilenet.org (with additional links)

Texas Inmate Families Association (TIFA)
P.O. Box 300220
Austin, TX 78703-0004
512-371-0900
www.tifa.org

Citizens United for Rehabilitation of Errants (CURE)
P.O. Box 2310
Washington, DC 20013
(For Texas: www.txcure.org)

Prisoner Express
127 Anabel Taylor Hall
Ithaca, NY 14853

Legal Services for Prisoners with Children (LSPC)
1540 Market Street, Suite 490
San Francisco, CA 94102
415-255-7036
www.prisonerswithchildren.org

Commission on Safety and Abuse in America's Prisons
601 Thirteenth Street, N.W.Suite 1150 South
Washington, DC 20005
www.prisoncommission.org

Children's Prison Arts Project
P.O. Box 130584
Houston, TX 77219-0584
713-520-7661
www.childrensprisonart.org

CORRECTIONS INFORMATION

National Institute of Corrections
U.S. Department of Justice
www.ncic.org

Bureau of Justice Statistics
U.S. Department of Justice
www.ojp.usdoj.gov/ojs

The JVA Institute
www.JFA-associates.com

JUSTICE CONCERNS

Justice Fellowship
P.O. Box 16069
Washington, DC 20041-6301
703-904-7312
www.justicefellowship.org

American Friends Service Committee
Criminal Justice Program
1501 Cherry Street
Philadelphia, PA 19102
215-241-7130
afscinfo@afsc.org

National Institute of Justice
Office of Justice Programs
810 7th Street NW
Washington, DC 20531
202-514-6235

National Organization for Victim Assistance
1757 Park Road NW
Washington, DC 20010
202–232-6682

The Sentencing Project
918 F Street NW Suite 501
Washington, DC 20004
202-628-0871

Mennonite Office on Crime and Justice
P.O. Box 500
Akron, PA 17501-0500
717-859-3889

Juvenile Justice Ministries Network of Texas
P.O. Box 765156
Dallas, TX 75376-5156
214-969-7834
www.jjmnt.org

The Innocence Project
100 Fifth Avenue, 3rd Floor
New York, NY 10011
212-364-5340
info@innocenceproject.org

Texas Criminal Justice Coalition
P.O. Box 301587
Austin, Texas 78703-0027
512-441-8123
info@criminaljusticecoalition.org

Bibliography

Abramsky, Sasha. *American Furies: Crime, Punishment, and Vengeance in the Age of Mass Imprisonment.* Boston: Beacon Press, 2007.

Anderson, Bernhard W. *Understanding the Old Testament.* Englewood Cliffs, NJ: Prentice-Hall, Inc., 1957.

Axtman, Kris. "A Flood of Parolees Hits the Streets." *The Christian Science Monitor,* December 2 (2002), lines 51–57. Accessed October 20, 2008. Online: http://www .csmonitor.com/2002/1202/p01s03-usju.html.

Baca, Jimmy Santiago. *A Place to Stand.* New York: Grove/Atlantic, Inc., 2001.

Barth, Karl. *Deliverance to the Captives.* London: SCM Press, 1961.

Beckner, W. Thomas, and Jeff Park, eds. *Effective Jail and Prison Ministry for the Twenty-First Century.* Euless, TX: A Coalition of Prison Evangelists Publication, 1998.

Bergner, Daniel. *God of the Rodeo: The Quest for Redemption in Louisiana's Angola Prison.* New York: Ballantine Books, 1998.

Bernstein, Nell. *All Alone in the World: Children of the Incarcerated.* New York: The New Press, 2005.

Blumenthal, Ralph. *Miracle at Sing Sing: How One Man Transformed the Lives of America's Most Dangerous Prisoners.* New York: St. Martin's Press, 2004.

Bogan, Louise. *The Blue Estuaries: Poems 1923–1968.* "Men Who Loved Wholly Beyond Wisdom." No Pages. Accessed October 22, 2008. Online: http://www.poemhunter .com/poem/men-loved-wholly-beyond-wisdom/

Bonhoeffer, Dietrich. *Letters and Papers from Prison.* New York: Touchstone, Simon & Shuster, Inc., 1997.

———.*Psalms: The Prayer Book of the Bible.* Minneapolis: Augsburg Publishing House, 1970.

Brueggemann, Walter. *Cadences of Home: Preaching among Exiles.* Louisville: Westminster John Knox Press, 1997.

———. *Finally Comes the Poet: Daring Speech for Proclamation.* Minneapolis: Fortress Press, 1989.

———.*Interpretation and Obedience: From Faithful Reading to Faithful Living.* Minneapolis: Fortress Press, 1991.

———. *The Message of the Psalms: A Theological Commentary.* Minneapolis: Augsburg Publishing House, 1984.

———. *Spirituality of the Psalms.* Minneapolis: Fortress Press, 2002.

———. *Texts That Linger, Words That Explode.* Edited by Patrick D. Miller. Minneapolis: Fortress Press, 2000.

Buechner, Frederick. *Telling Secrets.* San Francisco: HarperCollins Publishers, 1991.

———. *The Longing for Home: Recollections and Reflections.* San Francisco: HarperCollins Publishers, 1996.

Carder, Bishop Kenneth L. ". . . You Visited Me: The Call to Prison Ministry." *The Christian Century,* October (2006) 28.

Covert, Henry G. *Ministry to the Incarcerated.* Chicago: Loyola Press, 1995.

Bibliography

Crouse, Janice Shaw. "Finding Hope in Kate's Closet: One Woman's Efforts to Give Hope to Former Inmates." *Good News Magazine*, November–December (2004). Accessed October 16, 2008. Online: http://www.goodnewsmag.org/magazine/NovemberDecember/nd04Kates.htm

Davie, Donald. *To Scorch or Freeze: Poems about the Sacred.* Chicago: The University of Chicago Press, 1988.

Foucault, Michel. *Discipline & Punish: The Birth of the Prison.* New York: Vintage, 1979.

Franklin, H. Bruce. *Prison Writing in 20th Century America.* New York: Penguin Books, 1998.

Gibbons, John J., and Nicholas de B. Katzenbach. "Confronting Confinement." In *A Report of the Commission on Safety and Abuse in America's Prisons.* New York: Vera Institute of Justice, 2006.

Gordon, Robert Ellis. *The Funhouse Mirror: Reflections on Prison.* Pullman, WA: Washington State University Press, 2000.

Gorringe, Timothy. *God's Just Vengeance.* New York: Cambridge University Press, 1996.

Griffith, Lee. *The Fall of the Prison: Biblical Perspectives on Prison Abolition.* Grand Rapids: William B. Eerdmans Publishing Company, 1993.

Hallinan, Joseph T. *Going Up the River: Travels in a Prison Nation.* New York: Random House, 2003.

Hauerwas, Stanley. *Dispatches from the Front: Theological Engagements With the Secular.* Durham: Duke University Press, 1994.

———. "Matthew." In *Brazos Theological Commentary on the Bible.* Vol. 3. Grand Rapids: Brazos Press, 2006.

———. *Performing the Faith.* Grand Rapids: Brazos Press, 2004.

———. *The Peaceable Kingdom.* Notre Dame, IN: University of Notre Dame Press, 1983.

Herbert, George. "Bitter-Sweet." In *Praying with the English Poets.* Compiled and edited by Ruth Etchells. London: Triangle SPCK, 1990.

Hogan, Michael. *Letters For My Son.* Greensboro, NC: Unicorn Press, 1975.

Hopkins, Gerard Manley. *The Poems of Gerard Manley Hopkins.* Edited by W.H. Gardner and N.H. MacKenzie. New York: Oxford University Press, 1970.

Huber, John. *Last Chance in Texas: The Redemption of Criminal Youth.* New York: Random House, 2005.

Johnson, Jan. "Mary's Merciful Song of Justice." *Weavings* November/December (2002) 40.

Jones, Susan Pendleton, and L. Gregory Jones. "Worship, the Eucharist, Baptism and Aging." In *Growing Old in Christ.* Edited by Stanley Hauerwas, Carol Bailey Stoneking, Keith G. Meador, and David Cloutier. Grand Rapids: William B. Eerdmans Publishing Company, 2003.

Jones, W. Paul. *Facets of Faith: Living the Dimensions of Christian Spirituality.* Cambridge, MA: Cowley Publications, 2003.

Kersten, Phyllis. "Reaching Through the Bars." *The Christian Century*, September 26–October 3 (2001) 21.

Lampman, Lisa Barnes, ed. *God and the Victim: Theological Reflections on Evil, Victimization, Justice and Forgiveness.* Grand Rapids: William B. Eerdmans Publishing Company, 1999.

Logan, James Samuel. *Good Punishment? Christian Moral Practice and U.S. Imprisonment.* Grand Rapids: William B. Eerdmans Publishing Company, 2008.

Lowrie, Donald. *My Life in Prison.* New York: Mitchell Kennerley, 1912.

Bibliography

Lozoff, Bo. *We're All Doing Time: A Guide for Getting Free.* Durham: Human Kindness Foundation, 1985.

Magnini, Laura, and Harmon Wray. *Beyond Prisons: A New InterFaith Paradigm for Our Failed Prison System.* Minneapolis: Fortress Press, 2006.

Marshall, Christopher. *Beyond Retribution: A New Testament Vision for Justice, Crime and Punishment.* Grand Rapids: William B. Eerdmans Publishing Company, 2001.

Marty, Martin E. *A Cry of Absence: Reflections for the Winter of the Heart.* San Francisco: Harper & Row Publishers, 1983.

Merton, Thomas. *No Man Is An Island.* New York: Harcourt, Brace & Company, 1983.

Milton, John. *The Oxford Book of English Verse: 1250–1900.* "L'Allegro." Edited by Arthur Quiller-Couch, 1919. No Pages. Accessed October 17, 2008. Online: http://www.bartleby.com/101/310.html

Morgan, G. Campbell. "Songs in Prison." *Westminster Pulpit,* vol. 11. In *In the Shadow of Grace: The Life and Meditations of G. Campbell Morgan.* Compiled and Edited by Richard Morgan, Howard Morgan, and John Morgan. Grand Rapids: Baker Books, 2007.

Nietzsche, Friedrich. *Beyond Good and Evil: Prelude to a Philosophy of Future.* Translated and edited by Walter Kaufmann. New York: Modern Library, 1968.

Nouwen, Henri J.M. *The Wounded Healer.* New York: An Image Book-Doubleday, 1972.

Owens, Virginia Stem, and David Clinton Owens. *Living Next Door to the Death House.* Grand Rapids: William B. Eerdmans Publishing Company, 2003.

Reid, Sue Titus. *Criminal Justice.* 4th ed. Chicago: Brown & Benchmark, 1996.

———. *Criminal Justice.* 7th ed. Mason, OH: Atomic Dog Publishing, 2006.

Renaud, Jorge Antonio. *Behind the Walls: A Guide for Families and Friends of Texas Prison Inmates.* Denton, TX: University of North Texas Press, 2002.

Robinson, Marilynne. *Gilead.* New York: Farrar, Straus, and Giroux, 2004.

Ross, Jeffrey Ian, and Stephen C. Richards. *Behind Bars: Surviving Prison.* Indianapolis: Alpha Books, 2002.

Ross, Joseph. "On Looking at the Moon From Within a Prison." *The Other Side,* March-April (2001), 14.

Saliers, Don, and Emily Saliers. *A Song to Sing, A life to Live: Reflections on Music as Spiritual Practice.* San Francisco: Josey-Bass, 2005.

Skotnicki, Andrew. *Religion and the Development of the American Penal System.* Washington, DC: University Press of America, 2000.

Smarto, Donald. *Justice and Mercy: A Christian Solution to America's Correctional Crisis.* Wheaton, IL: Tyndale House Publishers, 1987.

Spitale, Lennie. *Prison Ministry: Understanding Prison Culture Inside and Out.* Nashville: Broadman & Holman Publishers, 2002.

Taylor, Mark Lewis. *The Executed God: The Way of the Cross in Lockdown America.* Minneapolis: Augsburg Press, 2001.

Texas State Historical Association. *Handbook of Texas Online,* s.v. *Handbook of Texas Online.* No Pages. Accessed July 3, 2006. Online: http://www.tshaonline.org/handbook/online/articles/TT/mdtva.html

Thomas, Dylan. *The Collected Poems of Dylan Thomas.* "Fern Hill." No pages. Accessed October 22, 2008. Online: http://www.poets.org/viewmedia.php/prmMID/15378

Vanier, Jean. *The Broken Body: Journey to Wholeness.* Mahwah, NJ: Paulist Press, 1988.

Westermann, Claus. *Praise and Lament in the Psalms.* Atlanta: John Knox Press, 1981.

Bibliography

Willit, Jim, and Ron Rozelle. *Warden: Prison Life and Death from the Inside Out.* Albany, TX: Bright Sky Press, 2004.

Worth, Robert. "A Model Prison." *The Atlantic Online*, November (1995). Accessed October 14, 2008. Online: http://www.theatlantic.com/issues/95nov/prisons/prisons.htm

Wynn, Jennifer. *Inside Rikers: Stories from the World's Largest Penal Colony.* New York: St. Martin's Press, 2001.

Zehr, Howard. *Changing Lenses: A New Focus for Crime and Justice.* Scottsdale, PA: Herald Press, 1990.

———. "Retributive Justice, Restorative Justice." In *New Perspectives in Crime and Justice: Occasional Papers.* No. 4. Akron, PA: Mennonite Central Committee Office of Crime and Justice, September, 1985.

Zimbardo, Philip. *The Lucifer Effect: Understanding How Good People Turn Evil.* New York: Random House Paperbacks, 2008. Zinn, Howard. *A People's History of the United States 1492– Present.* New York: HarperCollins Publishers, 2001.